CALIFORNIA POWER OF ATTORNEY HANDBOOK

CALIFORNIA POWER OF ATTORNEY HANDBOOK

with forms

John J. Talamo
Douglas Godbe
Edward A. Haman
Attorneys at Law

Sphinx Publishing
A Division of Sourcebooks, Inc.
Naperville, IL • Clearwater, FL

First Edition, 1998

Published by: **Sphinx® Publishing, A Division of Sourcebooks, Inc.®**

<u>Naperville Office</u>	<u>Clearwater Office</u>
P.O. Box 372	P.O. Box 25
Naperville, Illinois 60566	Clearwater, Florida 33757
(630) 961-3900	(727) 587-0999
Fax: 630-961-2168	Fax: 727-586-5088

Interior Design and Production: Shannon E. Harrington, Sourcebooks, Inc.

This publication is designed to provide accurate and authoritative information in regard to the subject matter covered. It is sold with the understanding that the publisher is not engaged in rendering legal, accounting, or other professional service. If legal advice or other expert assistance is required, the services of a competent professional person should be sought.

*From a Declaration of Principles Jointly Adopted by a Committee of the
American Bar Association and a Committee of Publishers and Associations*

Library of Congress Cataloging-in-Publication Data
Talamo, John.
    California power of attorney handbook : with forms / John J.
Talamo, Douglas Godbe, Edward A. Haman
       p.   cm.
    Includes index.
    ISBN 1-57071-360-X (pbk.)
    1. Power of attorney—California—Popular works.   2. Power of
attorney—California—Forms.   I. Godbe, Douglas.
II. Haman, Edward A.   III. Title.
KFC336.Z9T35   1998
346.79402'9—dc21   98-20201
                                                           CIP

Printed and bound in the United States of America.

Paperback — 10 9 8 7 6 5 4 3 2 1

CONTENTS

In General
Financial Power of Attorney
Special Power of Attorney for Financial Institutions
Durable and Springing Powers of Attorney
Durable Power of Attorney for Health Care (DPAHC)
Living Wills
Power of Attorney for Child Care
Who Needs a Power of Attorney

Finding the Law
Finding a Lawyer

In General
Mental Capacity Necessary to Execute a Power of Attorney
Recognition of Financial Powers of Attorney
Recognition of Health Care Powers of Attorney
Summing Up

Uniform Statutory Form Power of Attorney
Special Instructions for Agent
Selecting an Agent
Summing Up

Using Self-Help Law Books

Whenever you shop for a product or service, you are faced with various levels of quality and price. In deciding what product or service to buy, you make a cost/value analysis on the basis of your willingness to pay and the quality you desire.

When buying a car, you decide whether you want transportation, comfort, status, or sex appeal. Accordingly, you decide among such choices as a Neon, a Lincoln, a Rolls Royce, or a Porsche. Before making a decision, you usually weigh the merits of each option against the cost.

When you get a headache, you can take a pain reliever (such as aspirin) or visit a medical specialist for a neurological examination. Given this choice, most people, of course, take a pain reliever, since it costs only pennies, whereas a medical examination costs hundreds of dollars and takes a lot of time. This is usually a logical choice because rarely is anything more than a pain reliever needed for a headache. But in some cases, a headache may indicate a brain tumor, and failing to see a specialist right away can result in complications. Should everyone with a headache go to a specialist? Of course not, but people treating their own illnesses must realize that they are betting on the basis of their cost/value analysis of the situation, they are taking the most logical option.

The same cost/value analysis must be made in deciding to do one's own legal work. Many legal situations are very straight forward, requiring a simple form and no complicated analysis. Anyone with a little intelligence and a book of instructions can handle the matter without outside help.

But there is always the chance that complications are involved that only an attorney would notice. To simplify the law into a book like this, several legal cases often must be condensed into a single sentence or paragraph. Otherwise, the book would be several hundred pages long and too complicated for most people. However, this simplification necessarily leaves out many details and nuances that would apply to special or unusual situations. Also, there are many ways to interpret most legal questions. Your case may come before a judge who disagrees with the analysis of our authors.

Therefore, in deciding to use a self-help law book and to do your own legal work, you must realize that you are making a cost/value analysis and deciding that the chance your case will not turn out to your satisfaction is outweighed by the money you will save in doing it yourself. Most people handling their own simple legal matters never have a problem, but occasionally people find that it ended up costing them more to have an attorney straighten out the situation than it would have if they had hired an attorney in the beginning. Keep this in mind while handling your case, and be sure to consult an attorney if you feel you might need further guidance.

INTRODUCTION

This book is designed to enable you to prepare your own power of attorney or living will without hiring a lawyer. It will explain the different types of powers of attorney, guide you in deciding which type you need, and show you how to prepare one. Be sure to read "Using Self-Help Law Books" on page 1.

IMPORTANT NOTICE

Any time you give someone the power to make decisions for you regarding your finances or your health, you must do so thoughtfully and carefully. This book contains many warnings. They are not meant to deter you from the "do it yourself" method. The authors simply wish to emphasize the importance of what you are doing. As long as you understand each step you are taking, and get professional advice when you don't understand, you can accomplish many necessary and worthwhile purposes by doing it yourself. You will also save a considerable amount of money. A thorough reading of this book (maybe more than once) should save you time and money even if you decide to use a lawyer.

Creating a power of attorney is relatively easy. You must realize, however, that it can be a very powerful tool which can have far reaching effects. Some, such as the Power of Attorney for Health Care, are highly recommended. The financial powers are another matter. Be sure to read the warnings carefully before giving someone the right to control your money. This book will give you the information you need to decide what forms you need and how to fill them out. You may also want to visit your local law library to get more information. Chapter 3 will help you with this.

To complete the necessary forms you will need to read the general instructions in the main part of this book and look at the sample completed forms in appendix B. You may also want to read the actual California Statutes provisions in appendix A and use the information from any additional reading and research you do. If you need to refer back to this book for answers to specific questions, use the table of contents and the index to help locate the answers you need.

WHAT IS A POWER OF ATTORNEY AND WHO NEEDS ONE?

IN GENERAL

A power of attorney is simply a document giving someone permission to do something for you. It gives another person the legal authority to represent you and act on your behalf. This is necessary when some third person is asked to rely on that authority.

Of course, a power of attorney is not necessary every time someone does something for you. For example, if you ask me to get you a gallon of milk from the supermarket, I can do it without a power of attorney. I will be paying for it with cash at the time I get it, and the grocer has no concern about our arrangement.

It is an entirely different matter, however, if you ask me to go to your bank and borrow $2,000 in your name. The bank will want to be sure that you agree and are legally obligated to repay the loan, and they won't just take my word for it. The bank will want to protect itself, so it will require some kind of proof that you have authorized me to obligate you to repay the money. A power of attorney could provide the bank with the assurance it needs.

TERMS   To understand a power of attorney, it is necessary to know a few terms:

agent. The person who is given authority by a *power of attorney*.

attorney-at-law. A person who is licensed to practice law before state or federal courts. The term has no relationship to an *attorney-in-fact*.

attorney-in-fact. The person who is given authority by a power of attorney. This is another term for an agent. An attorney-in-fact does not have the power to represent anyone in court or to give legal advice.

durable power of attorney. A power of attorney which continues after the *principal* becomes incapacitated.

execute. To sign a legal document, thereby making it effective.

general power of attorney. A power of attorney which gives the agent very broad powers, generally to conduct all kinds of business and personal financial matters on behalf of the principal.

health care power of attorney. A special kind of power of attorney which gives the agent the authority to make decisions regarding the principal's medical care. The agent has power only in the event the principal is mentally unable to make intelligent decisions, or is unable to communicate his or her decisions

health care provider. A person who is licensed, certified, or otherwise authorized or permitted by the laws of California to administer health care in the ordinary course of business or the practice of a profession.

limited power of attorney. A power of attorney which limits the agent's authority to certain specific areas or actions.

living will. A document stating your desires in the event you become terminally ill and are not able to express your wishes. California's only authorized version is called the DECLARATION UNDER NATURAL DEATH ACT OF CALIFORNIA (Form 3).

power of attorney. A document that gives one person (the agent) authority to act on behalf of another person (the principal).

powers of attorney. The plural form of *power of attorney*. Also, the various specific authorities granted to an agent in a power of attorney.

principal. The person who executes the power of attorney, and thereby gives the agent the authority to act on his or her behalf.

special power of attorney. Another term for *limited power of attorney*.

special power of attorney for financial institutions. A power of attorney limited to one or more accounts or safe deposit boxes at a single financial institution.

springing power of attorney. A power of attorney which does not become effective until a certain event occurs, such as the incapacity of the principal.

Uniform Durable Power of Attorney Act. The law adopted in California and the majority of states which sets forth certain requirements for a *durable power of attorney*.

An example of how some of these terms are used is: "The principal executed a limited power of attorney, giving his agent the power to handle the sale of his house."

Although powers of attorneys can be effective during a subsequent incapacity of the principal (i.e., the *durable* power of attorney), powers of attorneys are never valid after the death of the principal [except for matters relating to the disposition of the principal's remains in the STATUTORY FORM DURABLE POWER OF ATTORNEY FOR HEALTH CARE (Form 2)].

In other words, if you give someone else a power of attorney, the authority created dies with you. Although a properly worded power of attorney can allow your agent to make estate planning decisions for you during your lifetime (e.g., make gifts, create or amend a living trust), the power of attorney is not effective to pass property after your death. To create a document to be effective after your death, consider alternatives such as living trusts, joint tenancies, Totten trust bank accounts, P.O.D.

("payable on death") accounts, or a will. See *How to Make a California Will*, by Kerri de Grosz Stenson and Mark Warda, available through the a local bookstore, or through the publisher by calling 1-800-226-5291.

In general, you need a power of attorney whenever you want someone else to act on your behalf in a matter of legal significance. Next, we will discuss the more common ways in which powers of attorney are used.

FINANCIAL POWER OF ATTORNEY

A financial power of attorney gives a person you designate the authority to act on your behalf in financial matters. This can be limited to one financial transaction, certain types of transactions, or all types of transactions. A financial power of attorney can include such things as transactions in real estate, personal property, stocks and bonds, banking, operating a business, borrowing money, entering into contracts, applying for government benefits, and making decisions regarding lawsuits.

You will need a financial power of attorney if you want someone to be able to act for you in some or all of your financial dealings. This is usually done when you have distant or numerous financial matters to attend to and cannot be there personally to transact all of the business. Chapter 4 will discuss the financial power of attorney in more detail.

A general power of attorney permits the agent to transact any and all business for the principal, although there are exceptions. California Probate Code Section 4264 requires specific authorization for certain acts by the agent, such as creating a trust or making a loan to the agent. Section 4265 sets forth those things which can never be authorized, such as creating a will (see sections 4264 and 4265 in appendix A for the complete list). In California, a power of attorney is general unless otherwise specified.

A *special* or *limited* power of attorney specifies or limits the agent's authority. For example, the agent may be given only the power to sign a deed transferring a specific piece of property of the principal to a specific person. The authors recommend limiting the agent's power whenever practical. There is no need to give your agent more power than is necessary to do the job.

Note: If you're still worried about the possibility of your agent abusing authority, you can have the agent purchase a surety bond (at your expense, of course). Surety bonds are explained in chapter 4.

SPECIAL POWER OF ATTORNEY FOR FINANCIAL INSTITUTIONS

California Probate Code Section 5204 provides for a special power of attorney for bank accounts and safe deposit boxes at a financial institution (e.g., bank, thrift, or credit union). If the only goal of the principal is, for example, to permit the agent to write checks from the principal's checking account, this type of limited power is recommended. The statute is reproduced in appendix A.

Most, if not all, banks will have their own form. Be aware that if you are trying to open an account or get a loan by using a power of attorney, the bank does not have to honor the power of attorney unless the principal is already a depositor or borrower (California Probate Code Section 4310).

Note: Be sure to make arrangements for deposits into the account, such as automatic deposit of social security checks, pension checks, etc. The bank can give you instructions to accomplish this.

Durable and Springing Powers of Attorney

A *durable* power of attorney is one that continues in effect even if you become disabled or incapacitated. Traditionally, a power of attorney ends if the principal dies or becomes incapacitated. *Mental incapacity* is when the principal cannot make an informed, intelligent decision. Since this is not always easily determined, a third party could refuse to honor the power of attorney if concerned that the principal might be incapacitated. Making the power *durable* removes the issue of the principal's capacity as a roadblock to the use of the power. Powers of attorney still end upon the principal's death. However, if the right words are used, the power of attorney can remain in effect if the principal becomes incapacitated. What words need to be used will be discussed in more detail in chapter 4. Any type of power of attorney can be made durable by the use of the right words. By its very nature, a power of attorney for health care is a durable power of attorney.

Section 4124 of the California Probate Code sets forth the language required for a durable power of attorney. Any of the following is acceptable:

(a) "This power of attorney shall not be affected by subsequent incapacity of the principal."

(b) "This power of attorney shall become effective upon the incapacity of the principal."

(c) Similar words showing the intent of the principal that the authority conferred shall be exercisable notwithstanding the principal's subsequent incapacity.

A power of attorney that will continue to be effective after the incapacity of the principal is created by (a). A power of attorney which will not become effective until the incapacity of the principal (a *springing* power of attorney) is created by (b).

A power of attorney can be made to become effective only upon a future event. This is called a *springing* power of attorney (i.e., it "springs" into effect upon the specified event). A power of attorney which becomes effective only upon the principal's incapacity is called a *springing* durable power of attorney.

A durable, or springing durable, power of attorney is often used between husband and wife, so that if one of them becomes incapacitated, the other can handle their financial matters. Although California law allows a non-incapacitated spouse to generally manage community property, management of the incapacitated spouse's separate property or the transfer of certain community property (e.g., sell the house), requires a court order (California Probate Code Sections 3000-3154). Having a durable, or springing durable, power of attorney makes the court order unnecessary.

DURABLE POWER OF ATTORNEY FOR HEALTH CARE (DPAHC)

A durable power of attorney for health care (DPAHC) is a special type of power of attorney allowing the agent to make decisions about the medical treatment for the principal if the principal is unable to make such decisions for himself or herself.

A health care power of attorney is most often used by a husband and wife, or close family members. Without a health care agent, doctors and hospitals may be reluctant to provide certain medical care if you are unable to give consent or help make decisions about various treatment options. More about health care powers of attorney will be discussed in chapter 5.

Living Wills

A living will is not a power of attorney. Unlike a health care power of attorney, no specific person is named in a living will to make your health care decisions. Instead, the living will expresses your desire not to have your life prolonged by artificial means. California's statutory version is called a Declaration Under Natural Death Act of California. The living will is explained in chapter 5 and the form is contained in appendix C (with a sample completed form in appendix B).

Power of Attorney for Child Care

California Family Code Sections 6550 and 6910 authorize a power of attorney for medical and dental care to whoever is caring for the minor. The agent must be an adult and the principal must be the parent, guardian, or caregiver as defined by California Family Code Section 6550. This section of the Family Code appears in appendix A, and a form in appendix C (with a sample completed form in appendix B).

The Family Code does not provide for payment for the treatment, and this should be arranged between the principal and agent, or directly with the health care provider (doctor or hospital). Emergency treatment cannot be denied by a hospital. However, non-emergency treatment could be denied if there is no suitable arrangement for payment. Be sure your agent has all of your insurance information.

Family Code Section 6910 provides for medical and dental treatment only. Principals may sometimes attempt to extend the power to provide decisions not related to the child's health. If your child is to spend an extended period away from you, you may want to consult a lawyer as to the best way to give authority to those who will be providing care. If you're leaving your child with a babysitter because you work long hours, or with someone for the weekend or a short vacation, the medical power should suffice, but see chapter 6.

Who Needs a Power of Attorney

Under what circumstances do you want or need a power of attorney, and are there alternatives?

Health care: Only a power of attorney for health care enables you to appoint a specific individual to make health care decisions for you. A court appointed conservator could also serve the purpose, but the time and expense of a court supervised conservatorship makes it a poor alternative to the STATUTORY FORM DURABLE POWER OF ATTORNEY FOR HEALTH CARE (Form 2).

Financial affairs: In today's world of fax machines, jet travel, and overnight delivery service, the temporary absence of the principal should not necessitate using a financial power of attorney.

However, during an extended illness or other circumstance when the use of a power of attorney is prudent, what kind should you use? We recommend that you use the most limited, both as to actions and time, that is practical.

Certainly there are other situations where a financial power of attorney may be desirable or necessary. For example, married couples may wish to execute springing durable powers of attorney in favor of each other, so that if one spouse becomes incapacitated, the other spouse can manage estate issues which would otherwise require a court order. Another time that a springing durable power of attorney may be necessary is when a principal wishes to make prior arrangements for the management of his or her financial affairs in case of incapacity.

CHOOSING AN AGENT
California law requires the principal of a power of attorney to be a competent, adult person. On the other hand, the agent may be a competent, adult person or a legal *entity*, such as a corporation, partnership, or trust. As a practical matter, you will probably appoint your spouse, a relative, or a close friend as your agent. However, if you have no one you want to act as your agent, you could contact a trust company. If they agree to

act as your agent, they will charge a fee for the service. They will also have their own forms for you to use. Their services may, however, be limited to business rather than personal matters, such as paying household bills.

ALTERNATIVES There are alternatives to a power of attorney, which may require the assistance of a lawyer. One may be the proper choice for you if a power of attorney is not suitable.

Conservatorship: Upon application, a court will appoint a conservator to care for someone who cannot take care of himself or herself. The drawbacks are costs and lack of privacy. The advantages are that the conservator is bonded, cannot enter into contracts or make gifts without court approval, and must file a periodic accounting for review by the court.

Conservatorship may be a better choice than a durable power of attorney when there is concern that the agent may be dishonest or, more commonly, that the agent may fail to keep adequate records or to properly conduct the principal's business.

Living trust: The living trust has become very popular in California. What it does and how to create one are beyond the scope of this book (See *Living Trusts & Simple Ways to Avoid Probate*, by Karen Ann Rolcik available at a local bookstore or by calling 1-800-226-5291.) If you have a living trust, it will serve many of the uses of a durable power of attorney. You must remember that only those assets which have been *funded* (put into the trust) can be managed by the trustee. IRAs, most pensions, and social security benefits are normally not funded. Also, problems such as personal care and income tax filing remain unsolved with a living trust. These problems can be solved by using a power of attorney along with your living trust.

Finding the Law and Finding a Lawyer

2

Finding the Law

CALIFORNIA
PROBATE CODE

Beginning with Section 4000 of the California Probate Code, you will find the law which regulates most powers of attorney in California. There are other laws regulating powers of attorney, but most of what you need is contained in these sections. Relevant sections, as well as other statutes, are contained in appendix A.

The Probate Code defines each type of power of attorney, and provides forms containing the acceptable language. These forms are not generally used by lawyers for all types of powers of attorney. They are, however, forms that you may use and are also helpful as a reference to guide you if a question arises.

This book contains forms that may be used for each type power of attorney. Appendix B contains sample forms filled out for fictional people. Appendix C contains the same forms blank.

LEGAL
ENCYCLOPEDIA

A *legal encyclopedia* is similar to a regular encyclopedia. You simply look up the subject you want (such as "Power of Attorney," "Principal and Agent," or "Agency") in alphabetical order, and the legal encyclopedia gives you a summary of the law on that subject. It will also refer to specific court cases, which can then be found in a *reporter*. On a national level, the two main sets are *American Jurisprudence* (abbreviated *Am. Jur.*) and *Corpus Juris Secundum* (abbreviated *C.J.S.*). You will also find three sets specifically for California called *California Jurisprudence* (abbreviated *Cal. Jur.*), *California Jurisprudence, Second Series* (*Cal. Jur. 2d*), and *California Jurisprudence, Third Series* (*Cal. Jur. 3d*). The Third Series contains the most recent information. In *Cal. Jur. 3d*, look for the chapter on "Agency," sections 26 through 33.

There are other sources of information about powers of attorney. Most of these sources relate to what is called *case law*, which refers to the interpretation of the Code by appellate courts. These sources include the following:

☞ **Digests.** A digest is a set of books that are arranged by subject, similar to a legal encyclopedia. But instead of giving a summary of the law, a digest gives summaries of various appellate court decisions interpreting that particular area of the law. Look for *West's California Digest*.

☞ **Case Reporters.** Case reporters, or reporters, are sets of books that contain the full written opinion of the appellate courts. You would need to use a legal encyclopedia or digest in order to find cases in a case reporter. There are primarily three case reporters for California court cases: California Supreme Court cases are found in *California Reports*. Cases for all California appellate courts are found in the *California Reporter*. Cases for appellate courts of California and fourteen other states are found in the *Pacific Reporter*.

If you have to interpret cases to decide if your power of attorney will be effective, consult a lawyer.

FINDING A LAWYER

Do you need a lawyer to prepare your power of attorney and, if so, how do you find one? In California, these questions are not difficult to answer.

This book is especially helpful since most instances when a power of attorney is used are not complicated legal matters. You're going to be out of town when the closing is to take place for the sale of your house. You wish to give your spouse a power of attorney to sign your name to the Grant Deed. What do you do?

You call the escrow company handling the transaction. They tell you what the lender or title insurance company requires. They may even have a form to give you.

You are in a retirement home and wish to have one of your children transact business at a bank for you. What do you do? You call the bank (or have your child call) and inquire as to the acceptable form and procedure.

The point is that many instances which call for a power of attorney involve an unbiased institutional third party that is familiar with the proper forms and procedures. If such a third party exists in your situation, look to it first for advice before preparing your form.

What about the other times? The common sense approach is best. Ask yourself how much confidence you have in your agent, and what's the worst that can happen if you don't do it right (or if you do it right)? If the worst that can happen isn't too bad, go ahead yourself. If the consequences are much more serious, find a lawyer.

Another consideration is the purpose and duration of the power of attorney. A power of attorney for a one-time transaction, such as signing a deed, is easily prepared. Suppose, however, you want to prepare a durable power of attorney for financial matters, a separate durable power for health care decisions, and wish to appoint separate agents (attorneys in fact) for each. Further suppose that you have a living trust. All these documents should be coordinated to avoid conflicting authority at some future time.

You get the idea. Treat yourself for a cold or to remove a splinter, but don't try to remove your tonsils. Common sense will tell you when an expert should be consulted. The forms in this book will allow you to create complex powers of attorney. If you decide to use a lawyer, a thorough reading of this book will give you the background to discuss the matter more intelligently. This will not only save time (money), but will help your lawyer do a better job.

You can use a lawyer in two different ways. The first way is to do the work yourself and ask a lawyer to give you an opinion as to its legality and effectiveness. The second way is to ask a lawyer to prepare the power of attorney for you.

Note: In this age of computerized forms it may actually take a lawyer longer to review the form you prepared than to prepare one.

Since most of the law controlling powers of attorney is found in the Probate Code, you know that a lawyer specializing in estate planning, trusts, and probate should be familiar with powers of attorney. The California Bar Association certifies specialists in certain areas of law. In order to become a specialist, a lawyer must have experience in the speciality and must take a test. A state certified specialist in the above mentioned areas of law can be found by contacting your county bar association. They have a list of all those who are certified and you can find someone convenient to you. The yellow pages and the internet are other possibilities.

Expect to pay $200 an hour for the specialist. The good news is that the work should be done quickly and correctly.

You can save money by being prepared. Make a list of things you wish to discuss and stick to it. Don't get involved in storytelling. A good lawyer will ask you for the necessary information.

Note: As stated earlier, most powers of attorney are not complicated legal matters. Unless estate planning is involved, any competent lawyer should be able to help you.

As with any person you hire, you should ask questions about costs and anything else about which you are unsure. If you don't like the answers or don't feel comfortable with that person, find another.

When you do settle on an attorney, be sure to be completely open and honest about your intentions. An attorney is bound by both privilege and confidentiality not to disclose anything you say. Only if the attorney knows exactly what you are trying to accomplish will your documents reflect those desires.

The Law Concerning Powers of Attorney

3

In General

The basics of the law concerning powers of attorney are fairly simple. By signing a power of attorney you are giving another person the authority to act on your behalf. Your power of attorney can give your agent broad powers, or it can limit him or her to specific actions.

The law provides that other people may rely on your power of attorney in doing business with your agent, so you will be bound by what your agent does through the power of attorney. This means that you had better have a great deal of trust in the person you select as your agent.

Mental Capacity Necessary to Execute a Power of Attorney

Under California law, a person must have "capacity to contract" in order to execute a power of attorney as the principal. For most people there has never been a determination as to whether they have the capacity to contract or not. However, a determination that a principal or agent did not have the capacity to contract will invalidate the power of attorney. By law, some persons do not have the capacity to contract, e.g., minors and some conservatees for some types of contracts (a *conservatee* is a person for whom the court has appointed another to handle financial matters). If there is any question whether the principal or agent has capacity to contract, then:

☞ A written medical opinion as to that issue at the time of the execution of the power of attorney may come in handy if the issue of capacity is subsequently raised; and,

☞ You should consult with an attorney before the execution of the power of attorney.

RECOGNITION OF FINANCIAL POWERS OF ATTORNEY

A major problem in some states is that third parties are reluctant to deal with the agent under a power of attorney. This is because there is no requirement that they must, and possible liability if they do.

California addresses the problem of recognition of financial powers of attorney in California Probate Code Sections 4300 to 4310. These sections set forth what the agent must do to require the third party to honor the power of attorney (Probate Code Section 4302 and the affidavit requirement of Probate Code Section 4305), and what the third party may rely upon to avoid liability for honoring an invalid power of attorney (Probate Code Section 4303).

An agent should be prepared to give the third party proper identification of the agent (such as a driver's license), signature examples of both the agent and the principal (e.g., canceled checks), a written statement containing the current and permanent address of the principal, and an affidavit executed by the agent stating that he or she does not have any knowledge of the termination of the power of attorney (Form 11).

Other problems that may arise are that third parties may have certain requirements before recognizing your power of attorney. For example, if your power of attorney pertains to real estate, a title company may insist that it be recorded in the county records. They may also require that the power is current (usually not more than six months to one year old). They may also insist that a certain form be used. Even though some of these requirements may not hold up in court, it is practical to make advance contact with third parties whenever possible and meet their requirements.

In California if the third party wrongfully refuses to recognize the agent's authority, the principal or the agent may bring a court action to compel the third party to accept the agent's authority. A losing third party may be liable for attorney fees (Probate Code Section 4306).

If you believe a third party is wrongfully refusing to accept your power of attorney, consult a lawyer. Since the other side is liable for attorney's fees, the other side will pay your lawyer if your position is correct.

An exception to a third party's legal obligation to honor a financial power of attorney permits a financial institution (e.g., bank, savings and loan, securities broker) to refuse to open a deposit account or lend money under a power of attorney unless the principal is already a depositor or borrower of that financial institution (Probate Code Section 4310).

RECOGNITION OF HEALTH CARE POWERS OF ATTORNEY

California law does *not* require a health care provider to accept the authority of the agent under a STATUTORY FORM DURABLE POWER OF ATTORNEY FOR HEALTH CARE (Form 2). Accordingly, if a health care provider will not accept an agent's power, the agent should arrange the principal's transfer to a health care provider who will recognize the agent's authority. If the principal has executed a valid DECLARATION UNDER NATURAL DEATH ACT OF CALIFORNIA (Form 3), a health care provider who refuses to withdraw medical life support when the patient's condition is terminal *must* transfer the principal to a health care provider that will abide by the directive. Failure to do so is a crime. (California Health and Safety Code Section 7190).

SUMMING UP

☞ The principal must have the *mental capacity to contract* in order to execute any power of attorney.

☞ The agent should be prepared to satisfy the concerns of third parties regarding the validity of a power of attorney.

- The financial power of attorney agent should be prepared to give the third party proper identification (e.g. driver's license), signature examples of both the agent and the principal (e.g., cancelled checks), a statement of the current and permanent address of the principal, and an affidavit executed by the agent that he or she does not have any knowledge of the termination of the power of attorney (Form 11).

- A legal action can be brought to force third parties to recognize a financial power of attorney, and the third party who wrongfully refuses to recognize a power of attorney can be required to pay the attorney fees of the agent or the principal who brings the legal action.

- There are no financial or criminal sanctions for a health care provider's refusal to recognize a durable power of attorney for health care. However, criminal sanctions can apply to a health care provider who refuses to abide by a patient's directive to be allowed to die naturally without the aid of artificial life support by executing a DECLARATION UNDER NATURAL DEATH

Act of California (living will), *and* fails to transfer that patient to a health care provider who will abide by the patient's directive. Accordingly, principals should execute a Declaration Under Natural Death Act of California (Form 3) besides a Statutory Form Durable Power of Attorney for Health Care (Form 2).

FINANCIAL POWERS OF ATTORNEY 4

The term *financial* power of attorney is not used in the code. It is, however, an accepted term used by lawyers and others to describe powers of attorney dealing with matters other than health care.

UNIFORM STATUTORY FORM POWER OF ATTORNEY (FORM 1)

Probate Code Section 4401 creates a statutory form of a financial power of attorney called the UNIFORM STATUTORY FORM POWER OF ATTORNEY (Form 1). The statutory form covers thirteen separate areas such as real estate, stocks and bonds, banking, business transactions, family maintenance, Social Security and Medicare, retirement, and taxes. Using an incorrect form may invalidate the financial power of attorney, therefore it is strongly suggested that you use only the statutory form in appendix C.

Be sure to read Form 1 completely and carefully, because it contains important instructions. To complete the UNIFORM STATUTORY FORM POWER OF ATTORNEY (Form 1):

1. Type in your name and address, and your agent's name and address on the lines indicated in the paragraph below the

NOTICE. You may designate more than one person to be your agent. If you do designate more than one person, be sure to type in the names and addresses of all agents. Selecting your agent is a very important matter. For more information about selecting your agent, see the subsection of this chapter titled "Selecting Your Agent."

2. Read the instructions on the form, then place your initials on the line before each power you wish to give your agent. As noted in the instructions on the form, if you want to give your agent the broadest power possible (a *general* power of attorney), you can simply initial line (N) which reads "ALL OF THE POWERS LISTED ABOVE." If you do not initial line (N), you are likely executing a *limited* power of attorney. Although the powers not given need only be left blank (not initialed), it is a good idea to put a line through each unused power as well as not initialing it. (See example in appendix B, Form A).

3. The next portion of the form, with the heading SPECIAL INSTRUCTIONS, allows you to specifically limit or extend the powers given. Examples of some possible special instructions are contained in the following subsection of this chapter.

4. On the second page of the form, the second paragraph reads: "This power of attorney will continue to be effective even though I become incapacitated." This sentence makes the form a durable power of attorney. If you do not want to make a durable power of attorney, you need to cross out this sentence.

5. If you designated more than one person as your agent, you need to complete the section titled EXERCISE OF POWER OF ATTORNEY WHERE MORE THAN ONE AGENT DESIG-NATED. All this requires you to do is type in either the word "separately" or the word "jointly" on the line after the phrase "If I have designated more than one agent, the agents are to act." If you type in "separately," it means that either agent can act alone.

If you type in "jointly," it means that all agents must agree on any course of action. If you have designated more than one agent and you leave this line blank, they will have to act jointly.

6. Next are places to fill in the date and your social security number, and to sign your name (which must be done before a notary public). On the third page, below the title CERTIFICATE OF ACKNOWLEDGMENT OF NOTARY PUBLIC, is the portion of the form the notary public will complete. (This section has been omitted on the sample Form A.)

Although copies of a power of attorney are not legally effective (under Probate Code Section 4307, only *certified* copies are legally effective), the statutory form allows third parties to rely upon a copy.

*The statutory financial power of attorney **must** have the principal's signature notarized.* The agent does not sign the statutory form power of attorney and need not even be aware of its execution.

SPECIAL INSTRUCTIONS FOR AGENT

As indicated above, there is a place on the first page of Form 1 for you to state any special instructions or limitations on the conduct or authority of your agent. Below are some examples of such special instructions and limitations.

SPRINGING POWER OF ATTORNEY

Many principals do not want their agent to have any authority unless they are incapacitated. Requiring that two medical doctors determine the incapacity acts to safeguard against a false determination of incapacity. The following language will make the power of attorney "spring" into legal effect only upon your incapacity (Probate Code section 4129).

> *Optional language:* "This power of attorney becomes effective only upon the incapacity of the principal who shall be incapacitated for purposes of this document if two licensed physicians

execute written opinions that the principal is physically or mentally incapable of managing his finances. No physician shall be subject to liability for executing such a medical opinion and the principal hereby waives any privileges that may apply to release of information included in such medical opinion."

The following powers are all designated in Probate Code Section 4264 and are more likely to be used in a *durable* power of attorney.

REVOCABLE TRUST AUTHORITY

☞ ***Optional language:*** "I grant my agent the power to create, modify, or revoke a trust."

Explanation: This power permits your agent to create a trust for your benefit, as well as to modify or revoke that trust. A living trust can accomplish the same thing as a will. Therefore, your agent could, in effect, write or rewrite your will. The purpose of this power is to permit your agent, if you are incapacitated, to do federal estate tax planning or probate avoidance. Because of the tremendous financial discretion given in this power, be very careful about granting it to your agent.

EXPIRATION DATE

☞ ***Optional language:*** "This power of attorney shall expire on *(date)*."

Explanation: Adding an expiration date makes sense if the power of attorney is only to be good during a planned absence or medical recovery. The automatic expiration date also helps protect you if you decide to revoke the power of attorney. The date automatically terminates your agent's authority without having to further notify third parties (which may be difficult).

ALTERNATE AGENT

☞ ***Optional language:*** "I appoint *(name of alternate agent)* as alternate agent if *(name of first nominated agent)* cannot act."

Explanation: You may wish to name a "back-up" agent. However, unless the first named agent dies or executes a resignation, it will be difficult for the back-up agent to prove to third parties that the first named agent is no longer acting.

TRUST
CREATION AND
FUNDING
AUTHORITY

☞ ***Optional language:*** "I grant my agent the power to fund, with my property, a trust created by me or created for my benefit by my agent."

Explanation: A living trust is only effective, for purposes of probate or conservatorship avoidance, to the extent assets are transferred into the living trust. This power allows your agent to transfer title to your assets to the living trust.

DISCLAIMER
AUTHORITY

☞ ***Optional language:*** "I give my agent the power to exercise the right of disclaimer on my behalf."

Explanation: A *disclaimer* basically says "I don't want the gift or inheritance." It might be exercised if the person receiving the gift or inheritance is already wealthy and doesn't want the gift or inherited asset to be subject to federal estate taxes in his or her own estate, or if the person receiving the gift or inheritance has creditor problems and doesn't want the asset to go to creditors. If a disclaimer is properly made, the gift or inheritance then goes to the person who would have received it if the person making the disclaimer had died before the person making the gift or bequest.

GIFT MAKING
AUTHORITY

☞ ***Optional language:*** "I give my agent the power to make gifts to himself or herself, or others from my trust or my estate."

Explanation: This power permits your agent to make gifts which might reduce the value of your estate, and save your estate federal estate taxes. This is not a power to give to your agent unless your agent is completely trusted by you, and even then you may want the power to be subject to approval by others you trust.

AUTHORITY TO
CHANGE
SURVIVORSHIP
INTERESTS

☞ ***Optional language:*** "I give my agent the power to create or change survivorship interests in property in which I have an interest."

Explanation: This power permits the agent to create or modify joint tenancies, etc., regarding your property. Again, this power permits your agent to rewrite your will or estate plan. This power should only be given when your agent is completely trusted, and even then you may want the power to be subject to approval by others you trust (see the subsection below on LIMITING AGENT'S AUTHORITY TO ACT.

AUTHORITY TO CHANGE BENEFICIARIES

☞ *Optional language:* "I give my agent the power to designate or change the beneficiary to receive any property, benefit or contract right on my death."

Explanation: This power permits the agent to make life insurance, pension, etc. beneficiary designations and thus gives the agent the power to rewrite the principal's will or estate plan. Obviously, this not a power to give to your agent unless he or she is completely trusted and even then you may want the power to be subject to approval by others you trust (see the subsection below on LIMITING AGENT'S AUTHORITY TO ACT.

LOAN AUTHORITY

☞ *Optional language:* "I give my agent the power to make a loan to the agent herein."

Explanation: Self explanatory. It is **not** recommended that you give this power to your agent.

LIMITING AGENT'S AUTHORITY TO ACT

☞ *Optional language:* "The above power may only be exercised upon written approval by *(name of family member or friend)*."

Explanation: Giving your agent any of the optional powers described above should be carefully considered. Many principals only give such powers to a spouse or trusted adult child, and many principals require approval of their agent's acts under the optional powers by other friends or family members of the principal.

Powers prohibited by law: Probate Code Section 4265 provides that an agent cannot be given the power to make, amend, or revoke the principal's will; or to consent to the principal's commitment to mental health facilities, convulsive treatment, psychosurgery, sterilization, or abortion (Probate Code Section 4722).

Note: The power to create a living trust essentially circumvents the prohibited power to make, amend, or revoke a will.

SELECTING AN AGENT

Be very careful about the selection of an agent. The agent may well have the power to financially ruin the principal. Simply appointing someone because he or she is "honest" is not enough. Your agent must also be fiscally responsible and have the ability, and the inclination, to keep excellent financial records of his or her actions. Naming one of your children, simply because he or she is "family," is not prudent. If the power of attorney is *durable*, then you, as the principal, may not later have the capacity to even know that your agent is mishandling your estate. You should strongly consider naming multiple agents and requiring them to act jointly. You should also consider requiring prior approval of some acts of your agent by others you trust (e.g., family members).

You may also want to consider having the agent(s) post a surety bond. The annual cost of such a bond is nominal when the protection it gives is considered (about 1% of the value of the bond amount, e.g., $1,000 per year for a $1,000,000 bond). If a surety bond is to be used, the principal should be directly involved in the negotiations with the bond company (surety bond companies can be found in the yellow pages or ask an attorney for the name of one). Many surety bond companies will require safeguards, such as periodic accounting by the agent to the bond company, to help protect the company from liability. Those protections for the surety bond company also protect the principal. Be sure that the surety bond cannot lapse or be terminated unilaterally by the agent.

California law permits corporations to act as an agent. Some professional trust companies will act as an agent under a power of attorney. Of course, a corporate agent will charge for its services. Further, trust companies may refuse to handle "personal finance" matters, such as paying household expenses.

Alternatives to the financial power of attorney described above would include a limited power of attorney over a single bank account, or the creation of a living trust. You may even want to select a court supervised conservatorship where your "agent" would be required to both post a surety bond and render periodic court accounting.

Furthermore, as between married couples, if one spouse becomes incapacitated, the other spouse can manage the family estate as to many day-to-day transactions *without* a power of attorney. What the non-incapacitated spouse cannot do is specified in Probate Code Sections 3000-3154. Those specified actions require a court order.

SUMMING UP

- ☛ Some printed forms for a financial power of attorney may not conform to California law. Use the California UNIFORM STATUTORY FORM POWER OF ATTORNEY (Form 1).

- ☛ Execute a *limited* power of attorney instead of a *general* power of attorney if you need only give your agent specific powers. If you want the power of attorney to be effective only in the event of your incapacity, execute a *springing durable* power of attorney.

- ☛ Consider some of the optional powers described above, but beware: you may be giving your agent the power to rewrite your estate plan or will. Consider completing your estate plan before you execute the power of attorney or making such powers subject to the written approval of other persons, such as trusted friends and family members.

- ☛ Be very careful whom you appoint as your agent. Consider having your agent post a surety bond as a condition of appointment. Consider naming co-agents who must act jointly.

- ☛ Literally "line out" the powers in the statutory form that you do not want your agent(s) to have.

- ☛ A financial power of attorney is a serious legal document. If you have *any* doubts or questions as to what you should do, you should consult with an attorney.

HEALTH CARE POWERS OF ATTORNEY 5

DURABLE POWER OF ATTORNEY FOR HEALTH CARE (DPAHC)

IN GENERAL

A durable power of attorney for health care (DPAHC) allows your agent to make medical care decisions concerning you if you are unable to do so. This includes the power to refuse or withdraw life-prolonging medical treatment. Obviously, a DPAHC is *durable*. Further, as you always have the right to direct your medical treatment if you have capacity (and the law presumes that you do), the power of attorney for health care is *springing* as well.

Regardless of your capacity, you have the right to object to (and thus overrule) medical treatment or the withholding of medical treatment necessary to keep you alive (Probate Code Section 4724). Also, your agent cannot:

☞ authorize your placement in a mental health facility, convulsive treatment, psychosurgery, sterilization, or abortion (Probate Code Section 4722).

☞ condone, authorize, or approve any mercy killing (Probate Code Section 4723).

☞ authorize any act which exceeds the limits of the DPAHC, nor do anything clearly against your best interests [Probate Code Section 4720 (b)].

Unlike a power of attorney for financial matters, the DPAHC extends beyond your death for purposes of authorizing the disposition of remains, autopsy, and organ donations (Probate Code Section 4720 (b), unless those powers are withheld from the agent.

STATUTORY DPAHC FORM

Probate Code Section 4771 authorizes a preprinted statutory form DPAHC (Form 2 in appendix C). This form is popular for two reasons. First, many health care providers will more readily accept a preprinted form over a typed form because they feel more secure that it conforms to the law and better protects them from liability. Second, if the form is not preprinted, a lawyer must sign a statement to the effect that the principal has been advised as to the consequences of the document (Probate code Section 4704). The STATUTORY FORM DURABLE POWER OF ATTORNEY FOR HEALTH CARE (Form 2) does not need to contain a statement executed by a lawyer (Probate Code Section 4772).

RECOGNITION OF DPAHC

First the good news: The DPAHC is readily accepted by most health care providers. This general acceptance reflects the health care industry's awareness of the purpose and effect of the DPAHC as well as the health care industry's awareness of its liability immunity for accepting a DPAHC. Now the bad news: There is no statutory requirement that a health care provider honor a DPAHC. In the event a health care provider refuses to recognize a DPAHC, the practical solution is for the agent to transfer the principal to a new health care provider who will honor the DPAHC.

USING THE STATUTORY FORM

The STATUTORY FORM DURABLE POWER OF ATTORNEY FOR HEALTH CARE (Form 2) is easy to fill out. To complete Form 2:

1. Read the extensive statutory warnings on the first page.

2. Insert your name and address on the line indicated in paragraph 1, and insert the name, address, and phone number(s) of your

agent on the lines after the words "do hereby designate and appoint." Below these lines is information about who may *not* act as your agent. Phone numbers are very important in providing a quick method of contact in an emergency. If there is an e-mail address for your agent, it should be included as well.

Selection of an agent. California law limits who may act as an agent. Health care providers, their employees, and operators of community and residential care facilities and their employees are barred from acting as DPAHC agents. [Probate Code Section 4701(a)]. However, relatives of the principal can be named as agent even if the relative fits in one of these categories. [Probate Code Section 4701(b)]. Married couples usually nominate each other, or a child, as agent. Common sense dictates that you should obtain the consent of your proposed agent before you nominate him or her, and you should give your agent a copy of your DPAHC. It is also advisable that you discuss your desires regarding your medical care with your agent.

One agent or co-agents? Whereas multiple agents in a durable power of attorney for financial matters can protect the principal from a single dishonest agent, multiple agents in a DPAHC merely add to the probability that the intent of the principal will *not* be followed, due to disagreement among the agents or the unavailability of an agent. For that reason the appointment of one agent is usually preferred.

3. You do not need to include a statement of desires in Paragraph 4(a), but it is recommended that you do so. If you do not want your life unnecessarily prolonged under life-support when there is no chance of recovery, you may want to insert something like:

```
I do not want my life to be unnecessarily and arti-
ficially prolonged with medical treatment if I have
an incurable and irreversible medical condition.
```

Although this language is vague, an intent is expressed which should give guidelines to health care providers and your agent.

Alternative language which might also be considered includes:

```
I want to die a natural death without having my life
unnecessarily prolonged by machines;
```

```
I want to die free of unnecessary pain and thus wish
medications to alleviate that pain even if the med-
ication might shorten my life.
```

```
I don't wish to be a financial or emotional burden
to my family.
```

On the other hand, if you want to have your life prolonged by medical life support, you might consider the following language:

```
I wish my life to be prolonged as long as possible
regardless of my physical condition or chance of
recovery.
```

4. In Paragraph 4(b) you might wish to limit the power given to your agent to make organ donations, authorize autopsies and/or make funeral arrangements. Examples might include:

```
I direct that no organ donations be made from my
body parts after my death.
```

```
I direct that the following body parts not be
donated after my death.
```

```
I direct that no autopsy be performed on my remains.
```

I direct that my remains be *(cremated or buried)*.

I direct the following funeral arrangements: *(funeral arrangements)*.

I have made written funeral arrangements with *(name of person or funeral home)*.

5. In paragraph 8 the principal can insert an expiration date. There is usually no reason to insert an expiration date. To avoid a date later being inappropriately added by someone else you should insert "Not Applicable."

6. Paragraph 9 permits the naming of alternate agents. If your first agent is killed or injured in the same accident which puts you in a coma, it might be wise to have an alternate named. Again, list all of the agent's phone numbers and e-mail addresses.

7. You may nominate a conservator in Paragraph 10.

8. In Paragraph 11 you, the principal, sign your name in the presence of two witnesses. Neither witness may be the agent, a health care provider, employees of a health care provider or operator of a community or residence care facility or any of their employees. Further, at least one witness may not be a relative or beneficiary of the principal's estate. One witness signs once and the other witness signs twice (the second signature states that the witness is not a relative or beneficiary of the estate of the principal). If you are a patient in a skilled nursing facility, the witness who signs twice must be a patient advocate or ombudsman and he or she must sign one more time at the very end of the document as the patient advocate/ombudsman. **Note**: The statutory DPAHC does *not* have to be notarized.

SAFEKEEPING THE DPAHC

Now, what do you do with the completed and executed document? *You make copies.* Although there is no statutory authority making non-certified copies legal, they are usually accepted by health care providers. The original DPAHC should be kept in a location that is known to those who are likely to be contacted in a medical emergency (such as your agent). However, as the DPAHC does not affect money, there is no reason to keep it in a safe deposit box. Copies should be given to your agent(s), your regular doctor(s) and your local hospital.

STATE REGISTRATION

You may register your DPAHC with the California Secretary of State. In theory, registration will enable a health care provider to obtain information concerning your DPAHC if necessary. Registration of the DPAHC is *not* required, and most people do not do so. The procedure for registration is outlined in Probate Code Sections 4800 through 4806.

NOTICE OF
HEALTH CARE
POWER OF
ATTORNEY
(Form 12)

The NOTICE OF HEALTH CARE POWER OF ATTORNEY (Form 12) may be carried in your wallet to assist in quicker notification of your DPHAC agent of your medical decision needs. Many people place this type of card with their organ donation cards. You may include the phone numbers of your physician or another non-agent if that person has a copy of your DPHAC or knows how to contact your agent. Note that there are two versions of Form 12, one to be used if you also have a living will.

PAYMENT OF
MEDICAL
EXPENSES

The DPAHC will not provide for payment of your medical treatment. If your agent under the DPAHC is also your agent under your financial power of attorney, there should be no problem. If not, you might consider giving the agent under your DPAHC a limited financial power to pay for the medical treatment.

LIVING WILLS

A living will is simply a document to cover the situation where you become terminally ill and are unable to express your wishes regarding the use of *life-sustaining treatment*.

California's only authorized living will is contained in the California Health and Safety Code, Sections 7184 through 7194.5, and is called a DECLARATION UNDER NATURAL DEATH ACT OF CALIFORNIA (Form 3 in appendix C). The use of any other form may not be valid.

Health and Safety Code Section 7193 provides that a DPAHC will prevail over a living will unless the living will specifically states otherwise.

Although considered to be superseded by the DPAHC, California's living will has an important purpose. If a heath care provider elects not to honor your intention, as stated in your DECLARATION UNDER NATURAL

DEATH ACT OF CALIFORNIA (Form 3), not to be sustained on life-support systems, it must transfer you to a health care provider who will abide by your directive not to be sustained on life support systems (Health & Safety Code Section 7190). Failure to make such a transfer exposes the health care provider to criminal sanctions. Such a transfer is not required under a DPAHC.

You must sign the DECLARATION UNDER NATURAL DEATH ACT OF CALIFORNIA (Form 3) in the presence of two witnesses, both of whom are *not* health care providers and one of whom is *not* entitled to any portion of your estate. The form does *not* have to be notarized. Further, if you are a patient in a skilled nursing facility or long-term health care facility, then one of the witnesses must be a patient advocate or ombudsman designated by the State Department of Aging. Accordingly, the statement at the bottom of the form should be completed, and if you are a patient in a skilled nursing facility, then the patient advocate or ombudsman who acts as a witness should be identified.

If you have executed a DPHAC, you should also complete the version of the NOTICE OF HEALTH CARE POWER OF ATTORNEY (Form 12) that includes the statement: "I have executed a Living Will," and carry it in your wallet or purse.

SUMMING UP

☛ The DPAHC is a "no-brainer." Sign one. There is no financial risk (except for the cost of the medical care directed by your agent). Your agent has power to direct your medical care only if you lack capacity and fail to object. The DPAHC should be executed whether you want life support in all situations or whether you want life support disconnected in certain, irreversible, terminable situations. Use the STATUTORY FORM DURABLE POWER OF ATTORNEY FOR HEALTH CARE (Form 2), or a printed form approved by your health care providers. Make copies of the executed DPAHC and give one to your doctor, hospital, nominated agent, and appropriate family members.

☛ You should also execute the living will, (the DECLARATION UNDER NATURAL DEATH ACT OF CALIFORNIA), as it gives legal assurance that you will be treated by a health care provider that will abide by your wishes not to be unnecessarily connected to medical life support systems. Use the DECLARATION UNDER NATURAL DEATH ACT OF CALIFORNIA (Form 3).

☛ To aid in notifying your agent, and to inform people if you also have a living will (DECLARATION UNDER NATURAL DEATH ACT OF CALIFORNIA), fill out the NOTICE OF HEALTH CARE POWER OF ATTORNEY (Form 12), and keep it in your wallet or purse.

Child Care Power of Attorney 6

A power of attorney for child care authorizes someone to make decisions regarding your child when you are not present to do so. This will usually be necessary if your child is going to live with a relative or friend, or will be on a prolonged visit to a relative or friend, who lives far away from you.

People send their children to live with someone else for a variety or reasons, including:

- making the child eligible for enrollment in a desired school system.

- sending the child to a distant private school.

- assuring adequate care for the child while the parent is working long hours, or must be "on the road" for business.

- assuring adequate care for the child during the parent's serious illness.

- sending a difficult child to someone better able to handle disciplinary problems.

- keeping the child away from an abusive parent.

- allowing the child a prolonged visit (eg., summer vacation) with a close friend or relative.

For whatever reason your child goes to live elsewhere, you will probably want that friend or relative to be able to enroll the child in school, camp or summer programs, sign permission slips for field trips, give consent to emergency or other medical care, and do whatever else is necessary for your child that would require parental consent.

When using a power of attorney for child care, be sure that it will accomplish your purpose. There is a statutory form which only provides for medical and dental treatment. This and other powers of attorney for child care are discussed below.

STATUTORY DURABLE POWER OF ATTORNEY FOR MEDICAL TREATMENT OF A MINOR

Section 6910 of the California Family Code provides for a DURABLE POWER OF ATTORNEY FOR MEDICAL TREATMENT OF A MINOR (Form 4), which also includes dental care. This form, however, does not authorize anything other than medical and dental care decisions. If you decide to use this form, show it to the doctor who will be most likely to treat your child. Make sure the doctor has no problem accepting the form, and that the hospital he or she practices at will accept it. How the doctor and hospital will be paid should also be discussed at that time. If you have health insurance for your child, give a copy of the insurance card or other insurance information (e.g., policy number, and the insurance company's name, address, and phone number) to the agent.

Form 4 is a durable power. You don't want your agent to lose authority because you become incompetent. This form is simple to complete, requiring the insertion of the appropriate names, dates, phone numbers, and addresses. A sample completed Form 4 is found in appendix B as Form D.

This form authorizes another adult to have the power to make medical and dental decisions for a minor. As the form is customarily used for a short period of time the insertion of a termination date is suggested. As most medical providers will attempt to reach the parent or guardian regardless of the form, it is suggested that phone numbers where the parent or guardian can be reached (e.g., name of hotel if on business trip) be included. This form does not have to be notarized or witnessed.

LIMITED POWER OF ATTORNEY FOR CHILD CARE

If your child will be living away from you for an extended period of time, you will want to authorize other purposes, such as enrollment in school, a summer camp, or summer recreation program. Check with the school, camp, or program, etc., to find if they will accept a power of attorney, and find out what type of form they would require.

The LIMITED POWER OF ATTORNEY FOR CHILD CARE (Form 5) may be of use in accomplishing your desires, but it should usually be used in addition to the DURABLE POWER OF ATTORNEY FOR MEDICAL TREATMENT OF A MINOR (Form 4). Use Form 4 to provide for medical and dental care, and Form 5 to give your agent other types of authority.

You may also want to consult a lawyer to see if another method, such as guardianship, may better suit your needs.

REVOKING A POWER OF ATTORNEY 7

As mentioned earlier, your agent will have the authority to bind you by what he or she does on your behalf. To guard against your agent getting out of control, you must have the ability to end his or her right to represent you.

There are several ways by which a power of attorney may be revoked. California Probate Code Sections 4150 to 4155 provide the rules for revocation and other terminations of the power. Section 4727 does the same for durable health care powers. Under these provisions, an agent's authority terminates in any of the following situations:

1. where the document itself calls for authority to end on a specific date. This is preferred when practical, as there is no confusion as to the termination of the agent's authority.

2. where the document calls for the power to terminate upon the happening of some event. For example, the power could terminate when the principal returns to the United States or is discharged from the military.

3. express revocation—The principal, either orally or in writing, informs the agent or a third party that the power is revoked.

4. revocation by operation of law—The power is automatically revoked, without any action being taken by the principal.

Examples of revocation by operation of law are the death of the principal or agent, or the divorce of a principal and agent who are husband and wife (if they remarry, it becomes effective again). For a non-durable power of attorney, the incapacity of the principal will also be a revocation by operation of law.

5. execution of a new power of attorney for health care—As a practical matter, revocation of a power of attorney for health care is not a major issue. Unlike a power of attorney for financial matters, a power of attorney for health care necessarily involves the presence of the principal. In that situation, the agent under a new power of attorney can easily dismiss the claims of an agent from a revoked power of attorney for health care. Further, as money is usually not a consideration of the agent, an agent has little incentive to pursue the revoked agency.

A financial power of attorney may be revoked by a court, upon appointment of a conservator (California Probate Code Section 4206).

FINANCIAL POWER OF ATTORNEY—NO REAL PROPERTY (Form 6)

The REVOCATION OF POWER OF ATTORNEY (Form 6) is used to revoke a financial durable power of attorney when the financial power of attorney does not concern any real property. To complete Form 6:

1. Fill in the principal's name and county of residence, the date of the power of attorney being revoked, and the agent's name on the lines indicated in the main paragraph.

2. The principal then needs to sign on the line marked "(principal)," fill in the date he or she signed, and fill in the principal's phone number and address on the lines indicated. The principal's signature does not have to be notarized or witnessed.

FINANCIAL POWER OF ATTORNEY— REAL PROPERTY (Form 7)

The REVOCATION OF POWER OF ATTORNEY (Form 7) is used to revoke a financial durable power of attorney when the principal owns real property which could be affected by the power of attorney (e.g., when the power of attorney is a general or a limited power of attorney that permits dealing with real property). To complete Form 7:

1. After the phrase "Recording Requested by," type in the name of the person who will be recording the form. This will often be the principal, but may also be an attorney, lender, or title insurer. After the phrase "When recorded return to," type in the name and address of where the form should be sent after it is recorded.

2. Fill in the principal's name and county of residence; the date of the power of attorney being revoked; the book, page number, and county where that power of attorney was recorded; and the agent's name on the lines indicated in the main paragraph.

3. In the space after the phrase "The address and legal description of real property affected by this revocation includes," the street address, city, and county of the real property should be inserted, along with the legal description. If the space on this form is inadequate to insert the legal description, then the street address, city, and county should be inserted in the space provided with the added note "see Exhibit A for legal description," and the legal description should be typed on a separate sheet of paper, which is titled "Exhibit A" and attached to the REVOCATION OF POWER OF ATTORNEY (Form 7). The Exhibit A should also include the street address of the subject real property.

4. The principal then needs to sign *before a notary public* on the line marked "(principal)," and fill in the date he or she signed. The notary will complete the bottom portion of the form.

If real property affected by the REVOCATION OF POWER OF ATTORNEY (Form 7) exists in more than one county, then a separate REVOCATION OF POWER OF ATTORNEY (Form 7) should be executed for each county.

The REVOCATION OF POWER OF ATTORNEY (Form 7) should be recorded in the county in which the real property is situated. To be recorded, the it must be notarized.

POWER OF
ATTORNEY FOR
HEALTH CARE
(Form 8)

The REVOCATION OF POWER OF ATTORNEY FOR HEALTH CARE (Form 8) can be used to revoke a health care durable power of attorney. To complete Form 8:

1. Fill in the principal's name and county of residence, the date of the DPAHC being revoked, and the agent's name on the lines indicated in the main paragraph.

2. The principal then needs to sign on the line marked "(principal)," fill in the date he or she signed, and fill in the principal's phone number and address on the lines indicated. The principal's signature does not have to be notarized or witnessed.

Note: The execution of a new DPAHC acts as an automatic revocation of the prior DPAHC. If a new DPAHC is executed, then the delivery of it to the prior agent and to the appropriate health care providers will render the execution of Form 8 unnecessary.

POWER OF
ATTORNEY FOR
MEDICAL
TREATMENT OF
A MINOR
(Form 9)

The REVOCATION OF POWER OF ATTORNEY FOR MEDICAL TREATMENT OF A MINOR (Form 9) can be used to revoke a DURABLE POWER OF ATTORNEY FOR MEDICAL TREATMENT OF A MINOR (Form 4). To complete Form 9:

1. In the first paragraph, fill in the name of the child and his or her birthdate on the lines indicated.

2. The open space after designation of the minor's name and age is to be used when there are multiple minors involved.

3. In the second paragraph, fill in the date of the DURABLE POWER OF ATTORNEY FOR MEDICAL TREATMENT OF A MINOR being revoked, and the name of the agent on the lines indicated.

4. The principal then needs to sign on the line marked "(principal)," fill in the date he or she signed, and fill in the principal's phone number and address on the lines indicated. The principal's signature does not have to be notarized or witnessed.

This revocation revokes the document itself, thus the power of alternate agents is also revoked. The principal's signature does not have to be notarized or witnessed. As such powers of attorney usually have an early expiration date (as they are used for vacations and other short periods of time) the execution of this form may not be necessary. A copy of the REVOCATION OF POWER OF ATTORNEY FOR MEDICAL TREATMENT OF A MINOR should be given to the agent(s) and forwarded to any appropriate health care providers to notify them of the revocation of the agent's power.

LIMITED POWER OF ATTORNEY FOR CHILD CARE (Form 10)

The REVOCATION OF LIMITED POWER OF ATTORNEY FOR CHILD CARE (Form 10) can be used to revoke a LIMITED POWER OF ATTORNEY FOR CHILD CARE (Form 5), or some similar power of attorney. To complete Form 10, follow the instructions for completing Form 9 above. If the power of attorney you are revoking is not titled "Limited Power of Attorney for Child Care," you will need to re-type this form substituting the title of the document you are revoking.

NOTICE REQUIREMENTS

After you have executed a revocation form, you will need to notify your agent and other appropriate third parties of your revocation. The burden to notify third parties of the revocation rests with the principal. Whom you need to notify may depend upon the type of power of attorney you have revoked.

Revocation of Financial Powers of Attorney. In addition to notifying your agent, you will need to notify any third parties with whom your agent has conducted business on your behalf. Notifying your agent of the revocation will not relieve you of liability to third parties dealing with your agent after you revoked, unless the third parties know of the revocation.

Revocation of Power of Attorney for Health Care. For a DPAHC, a copy of the REVOCATION OF POWER OF ATTORNEY FOR HEALTH CARE (Form 8) should be given to the agent(s), and forwarded to appropriate health care providers to notify them of the revocation of the agent's power. Upon receiving notice of revocation, a health care provider is required to enter the revocation in the principal's medical records and make a reasonable effort to notify the agent of the revocation.

Revocation of Power of Attorney for Medical Treatment of a Minor or ***Revocation of Limited Power of Attorney for Child Care.*** A copy of the REVOCATION OF POWER OF ATTORNEY FOR MEDICAL TREATMENT OF A MINOR (Form 9), or REVOCATION OF LIMITED POWER OF ATTORNEY FOR CHILD CARE (Form 10), should be given to the agent(s) and to appropriate third parties (e.g., doctors, hospitals, school, summer camp) to notify them of the revocation of the agent's power.

Appendix A
California Statutes

This appendix contains the text of various provisions of the *California Codes* concerning powers of attorney and living wills, except for the forms themselves which are found in appendix C. These provisions are from the Probate Code, Health and Safety Code, and Family Code.

Where a form has been deleted you will find the notation "*[See Form ___ in appendix B and Form ___ in appendix C].*" The numbers at the beginning of each provision are the section numbers.

As laws can change each year, be sure you have reviewed the most current version of the *California Codes*.

PROBATE CODE

SECTIONS 4000-4034

§ 4000. Short title; power of attorney law.

This division may be cited as the Power of Attorney Law.

§ 4001. Short title; uniform durable power of attorney act.

Sections 4124, 4125, 4126, 4127, 4206, 4304, and 4305 may be cited as the Uniform Durable Power of Attorney Act.

§ 4010. Definitions.

Unless the provision or context otherwise requires, the definitions in this chapter govern the construction of this division.

§ 4014. Attorney-in-fact.

(a) "Attorney-in-fact" means a person granted authority to act for the principal in a power of attorney, regardless of whether the person is known as an attorney-in-fact or agent, or by some other term.

(b) "Attorney-in-fact" includes a successor or alternate attorney-in-fact and a person delegated authority by an attorney-in-fact.

§ 4018. Durable power of attorney.

"Durable power of attorney" means a power of attorney that satisfies the requirements for durability provided in Section 4124.

§ 4022. Power of attorney.

"Power of attorney" means a written instrument, however denominated, that is executed by a natural person having the capacity to contract and that grants authority to an attorney-in-fact. A power of attorney may be durable or nondurable.

§ 4026. Principal.

"Principal" means a natural person who executes a power of attorney.

§ 4030. Springing power of attorney.

"Springing power of attorney" means a power of attorney that by its terms becomes effective at a specified future time or on the occurrence of a specified future event or contingency, including, but not limited to, the subsequent incapacity of the principal. A springing power of attorney may be a durable power of attorney or a nondurable power of attorney.

§ 4034. Third person.

"Third person" means any person other than the principal or attorney-in-fact.

SECTIONS 4050-4054

§ 4050. Application of division.

(a) This division applies to the following:

(1) Durable powers of attorney.

(2) Statutory form powers of attorney under Part 3 (commencing with Section 4400).

(3) Durable powers of attorney for health care under Part 4 (commencing with Section 4600).

(4) Any other power of attorney that incorporates or refers to this division or the provisions of this division.

(b) This division does not apply to the following:

(1) A power of attorney to the extent that the authority of the attorney-in-fact is coupled with an interest in the subject of the power of attorney.

(2) Reciprocal or interinsurance exchanges and their contracts, subscribers, attorneys-in-fact, agents, and representatives.

(3) A proxy given by an attorney-in-fact to another person to exercise voting rights.

(c) This division is not intended to affect the validity of any instrument or arrangement that is not described in subdivision (a).

§ 4051. Agency law; application.

Except where this division provides a specific rule, the general law of agency, including Article 2 (commencing with Section 2019) of Chapter 2 of Title 6 of, and Title 9 (commencing with Section 2295) of, Part 4 of Division 3 of the Civil Code, applies to powers of attorney.

§ 4052. Application of power of attorney law; conditions; change in domicile; removal of property.

(a) If a power of attorney provides that the Power of Attorney Law of this state governs the power of attorney or otherwise indicates the principal's intention that the Power of Attorney Law of this state governs the power of attorney, this division governs the power of attorney and applies to acts and transactions of the attorney-in-fact in this state or outside this state where any of the following conditions is satisfied:

(1) The principal or attorney-in-fact was domiciled in this state when the principal executed the power of attorney.

(2) The authority conferred on the attorney-in-fact relates to property, acts, or transactions in this state.

(3) The acts or transactions of the attorney-in-fact occurred or were intended to occur in this state.

(4) The principal executed the power of attorney in this state.

(5) There is otherwise a reasonable relationship between this state and the subject matter of the power of attorney.

(b) If subdivision (a) does not apply to the power of attorney, this division governs the power of attorney and applies to the acts and transactions of the attorney-in-fact in this state where either of the following conditions is satisfied:

(1) The principal was domiciled in this state when the principal executed the power of attorney.

(2) The principal executed the power of attorney in this state.

(c) A power of attorney described in this section remains subject to this division despite a change in domicile of the principal or the attorney-in-fact, or the removal from this state of property that was the subject of the power of attorney.

§ 4053. Durable power of attorney executed in another state; validity.

A durable power of attorney executed in another state or jurisdiction in compliance with the law of that state or jurisdiction or the law of this state is valid and enforceable in this state to the same extent as a durable power of attorney executed in this state, regardless of whether the principal is a domiciliary of this state.

§ 4054. Execution date; application of division; proceedings; validity of previously executed power

Except as otherwise provided by statute:

(a) On and after January 1, 1995, this division applies to all powers of attorney regardless of whether they were executed before, on, or after January 1, 1995.

(b) This division applies to all proceedings concerning powers of attorney commenced on or after January 1, 1995.

(c) This division applies to all proceedings concerning powers of attorney commenced before January 1, 1995, unless the court determines that application of a particular provision of this division would substantially interfere with the effective conduct of the proceedings or the rights of the parties and other interested persons, in which case the particular provision of this division does not apply and prior law applies.

(d) Nothing in this division affects the validity of a power of attorney executed before January 1, 1995, that was valid under prior law.

SECTIONS 4100-4102

§ 4100. Application of part.

This part applies to all powers of attorney under this division, subject to any special rules applicable to statutory form powers of attorney under Part 3 (commencing with Section 4400) or durable powers of attorney for health care under Part 4 (commencing with Section 4600).

§ 4101. Principal's power to limit application of statute; express statements; inconsistent rules; exclusions.

(a) Except as provided in subdivision (b), the principal may limit the application of any provision of this division by an express statement in the power of attorney or by providing an inconsistent rule in the power of attorney.

(b) A power of attorney may not limit either the application of a statute specifically providing that it is not subject to limitation in the power of attorney or a statute concerning any of the following:

(1) Warnings or notices required to be included in a power of attorney.

(2) Operative dates of statutory enactments or amendments.

(3) Execution formalities.

(4) Qualifications of witnesses.

(5) Qualifications of attorneys-in-fact.

(6) Protection of third persons from liability.

§ 4102. Printed form of durable power of attorney; sale or distribution; advise of legal counsel; validity.

Notwithstanding Section 4128:

(a) Except as provided in subdivision (b), on and after January 1, 1995, a printed form of a durable power of attorney may be sold or otherwise distributed if it satisfies the requirements of former Section 2510.5 of the Civil Code.

(b) A printed form of a durable power of attorney printed on or after January 1, 1986, that is sold or otherwise distributed in this state for use by a person who does not have the advice of legal counsel shall comply with former Section 2510 of the Civil Code or with Section 4128 of this code.

(c) A durable power of attorney executed on or after January 1, 1995, using a printed form that complies with subdivision (b) of former Section 2400 of the Civil Code, as enacted by Chapter 511 of the Statutes of 1981, or with former Section 2510 of the Civil Code, is as valid as if it had been executed using a printed form that complies with Section 4128 of this code.

SECTIONS 4120-4130

§ 4120. Execution; capacity.

A natural person having the capacity to contract may execute a power of attorney.

§ 4121. Legal sufficiency; conditions.

A power of attorney is legally sufficient if all of the following requirements are satisfied:

(a) The power of attorney contains the date of its execution.

(b) The power of attorney is signed either

(1) by the principal or

(2) in the principal's name by some other person in the principal's presence and at the principal's direction.

(c) The power of attorney is either (1) acknowledged before a notary public or (2) signed by at least two witnesses who satisfy the requirements of Section 4122.

§ 4122. Witnesses; qualifications; duties.

If the power of attorney is signed by witnesses, as provided in Section 4121, the following requirements shall be satisfied:

(a) The witnesses shall be adults.

(b) The attorney-in-fact may not act as a witness.

(c) Each witness signing the power of attorney shall witness either the signing of the instrument by the principal or the principal's acknowledgment of the signature or the power of attorney.

(d) In the case of a durable power of attorney for health care, the additional requirements of Section 4701.

§ 4123. Authority granted to attorney-in-fact; lawful subjects and purposes; property; personal care; health care.

(a) In a power of attorney, a principal may grant authority to an attorney-in-fact to act on the principal's behalf with respect to all lawful subjects and purposes or with respect to one or more express subjects or purposes. The attorney-in-fact may be granted authority with regard to the principal's property, personal care, health care, or any other matter.

(b) With regard to property matters, a power of attorney may grant authority to make decisions concerning all or part of the principal' s real and personal property, whether owned by the principal at the time of the execution of the power of attorney or thereafter acquired or whether located in this state or elsewhere, without the need for a description of each item or parcel of property.

(c) With regard to personal care, a power of attorney may grant authority to make decisions relating to the personal care of the principal, including, but not limited to, determining where the principal will live, providing meals, hiring household employees, providing transportation, handling mail, and arranging recreation and entertainment.

(d) With regard to health care, a power of attorney may grant authority to make health care decisions, both before and after the death of the principal, as provided in Part 4 (commencing with Section 4600).

§ 4124. Durable power of attorney; required language.

A durable power of attorney is a power of attorney by which a principal designates another person as attorney-in-fact in writing and the power of attorney contains any of the following statements:

(a) "This power of attorney shall not be affected by subsequent incapacity of the principal."

(b) "This power of attorney shall become effective upon the incapacity of the principal."

(c) Similar words showing the intent of the principal that the authority conferred shall be exercisable notwithstanding the principal's subsequent incapacity.

§ 4125. Incapacity of principal; acts of attorney-in-fact.

All acts done by an attorney-in-fact pursuant to a durable power of attorney during any period of incapacity of the principal have the same effect and inure to the benefit of and bind the principal and the principal's successors in interest as if the principal had capacity.

§ 4126. Nomination of conservator or guardian; protective proceedings.

(a) A principal may nominate, by a durable power of attorney, a conservator of the person or estate or both, or a guardian of the person or estate or both, for consideration by the court if protective proceedings for the principal's person or estate are thereafter commenced.

(b) If the protective proceedings are conservatorship proceedings in this state, the nomination has the effect provided in Section 1810 and the court shall give effect to the most recent writing executed in accordance with Section 1810, whether or not the writing is a durable power of attorney.

§ 4127. Termination of power of attorney; lapses of time.

Unless a power of attorney states a time of termination, the authority of the attorney-in-fact is exercisable notwithstanding any lapse of time since execution of the power of attorney.

§ 4128. Warning statement; notice to person executing durable power of attorney.

(a) Subject to subdivision (b), a printed form of a durable power of attorney that is sold or otherwise distributed in this state for use by a person who does not have the advice of legal counsel shall contain, in not less than 10-point boldface type or a reasonable equivalent thereof, the following warning statement:

Notice to Person Executing Durable

Power of Attorney

A durable power of attorney is an important legal document. By signing the durable power of attorney, you are authorizing another person to act for you, the principal. Before you sign this durable power of attorney, you should know these important facts:

Your agent (attorney-in-fact) has no duty to act unless you and your agent agree otherwise in writing.

This document gives your agent the powers to manage, dispose of, sell, and convey your real and personal property, and to use your property as security if your agent borrows money on your behalf.

Your agent will have the right to receive reasonable payment for services provided under this durable power of attorney unless you provide otherwise in this power of attorney.

The powers you give your agent will continue to exist for your entire lifetime, unless you state that the durable power of attorney will last for a shorter period of time or unless you otherwise terminate the durable power of attorney. The powers you give your agent in this durable power of attorney will continue to exist even if you can no longer make your own decisions respecting the management of your property.

You can amend or change this durable power of attorney only by executing a new durable power of attorney or by executing an amendment through the same formalities as an original. You have the right to revoke or terminate this durable power of attorney at any time, so long as you are competent.

This durable power of attorney must be dated and must be acknowledged before a notary public or signed by two witnesses. If it is signed by two witnesses, they must witness either (1) the signing of the power of attorney or (2) the principal's signing or acknowledgment of his or her signature. A durable power of attorney that may affect real property should be acknowledged before a notary public so that it may easily be recorded.

You should read this durable power of attorney carefully. When effective, this durable power of attorney will give your agent the right to deal with property that you now have or might acquire in the future. The durable power of attorney is important to you. If you do not understand the durable power of attorney, or any provision of it, then you should obtain the assistance of an attorney or other qualified person.

(b) Nothing in subdivision (a) invalidates any transaction in which a third person relied in good faith on the authority created by the durable power of attorney.

(c) This section does not apply to the following:

(1) A statutory form power of attorney under Part 3 (commencing with Section 4400).

(2) A durable power of attorney for health care under Part 4 (commencing with Section 4600).

§ 4129. Springing power of attorney.

(a) In a springing power of attorney, the principal may designate one or more persons who, by a written declaration under penalty of perjury, have the power to determine conclusively that the specified event or contingency has occurred. The principal may designate the attorney-in-fact or another person to perform this function, either alone or jointly with other persons.

(b) A springing power of attorney containing the designation described in subdivision (a) becomes effective when the person or persons designated in the power of attorney execute a written declaration under penalty of perjury that the specified event or contingency has occurred, and any person may act in reliance on the written declaration without liability to the principal or to any other person, regardless of whether the specified event or contingency has actually occurred.

(c) This section applies to a power of attorney whether executed before, on, or after January 1, 1991, if the power of attorney contains the designation described in subdivision (a).

(d) This section does not provide the exclusive method by which a power of attorney may be limited to take effect on the occurrence of a specified event or contingency.

§ 4130. Multiple powers of attorney; inconsistencies.

(a) If a principal grants inconsistent authority to one or more attorneys-in-fact in two or more powers of attorney, the authority granted last controls to the extent of the inconsistency.

(b) This section is not subject to limitation in the power of attorney.

SECTIONS 4150-4155

§ 4150. Modifications; notice.

(a) A principal may modify a power of attorney as follows:

(1) In accordance with the terms of the power of attorney.

(2) By an instrument executed in the same manner as a power of attorney may be executed.

(b) An attorney-in-fact or third person who does not have notice of the modification is protected from liability as provided in Chapter 5 (commencing with Section 4300).

§ 4151. Revocation; notice.

(a) A principal may revoke a power of attorney as follows:

(1) In accordance with the terms of the power of attorney.

(2) By a writing. This paragraph is not subject to limitation in the power of attorney.

(b) An attorney-in-fact or third person who does not have notice of the revocation is protected from liability as provided in Chapter 5 (commencing with Section 4300).

§ 4152. Termination of authority; triggering events; notice.

(a) Subject to subdivision (b), the authority of an attorney-in-fact under a power of attorney is terminated by any of the following events:

(1) In accordance with the terms of the power of attorney.

(2) Extinction of the subject or fulfillment of the purpose of the power of attorney.

(3) Revocation of the attorney-in-fact's authority, as provided in Section 4153.

(4) Death of the principal, except as to specific authority permitted by statute to be exercised after the principal's death.

(5) Removal of the attorney-in-fact.

(6) Resignation of the attorney-in-fact.

(7) Incapacity of the attorney-in-fact, except that a temporary incapacity suspends the attorney-in-fact's authority only during the period of the incapacity.

(8) Dissolution or annulment of the marriage of the attorney-in-fact and principal, as provided in Section 4154.

(9) Death of the attorney-in-fact.

(b) An attorney-in-fact or third person who does not have notice of an event that terminates the power of attorney or the authority of an attorney-in-fact is protected from liability as provided in Chapter 5 (commencing with Section 4300).

§ 4153. Revocation of authority; methods; notice.

(a) The authority of an attorney-in-fact under a power of attorney may be revoked as follows:

(1) In accordance with the terms of the power of attorney.

(2) Where the principal informs the attorney-in-fact orally or in writing that the attorney-in-fact's authority is revoked or when and under what circumstances it is revoked. This paragraph is not subject to limitation in the power of attorney.

(3) Where the principal's legal representative, with approval of the court as provided in Section 4206, informs the attorney-in-fact in writing that the attorney-in-fact's authority is revoked or when and under what circumstances it is revoked. This paragraph is not subject to limitation in the power of attorney.

(b) An attorney-in-fact or third person who does not have notice of the revocation is protected from liability as provided in Chapter 5 (commencing with Section 4300).

§ 4154. Dissolution or annulment of principal's marriage to attorney-in-fact; revocation; revival.

(a) If after executing a power of attorney the principal's marriage to the attorney-in-fact is dissolved or annulled, the principal's designation of the former spouse as an attorney-in-fact is revoked.

(b) If the attorney-in-fact's authority is revoked solely by subdivision (a), it is revived by the principal's remarriage to the attorney-in-fact.

§ 4155. Incapacity of principal under a nondurable power of attorney; notice

(a) Subject to subdivision (b), the authority of an attorney-in-fact under a nondurable power of attorney is terminated by the incapacity of the principal to contract.

(b) An attorney-in-fact or third person who does not have notice of the incapacity of the principal is protected from liability as provided in Chapter 5 (commencing with Section 4300).

(c) This section is not subject to limitation in the power of attorney.

SECTIONS 4200-4207

§ 4200. Capacity to contract.

Only a person having the capacity to contract is qualified to act as an attorney-in-fact.

§ 4201. Designation of unqualified person; immunities of third persons; duties.

Designating an unqualified person as an attorney-in-fact does not affect the immunities of third persons nor relieve the unqualified person of any applicable duties to the principal or the principal's successors.

§ 4202. Multiple attorneys-in-fact; action; vacancy; absence, illness or incapacity; liability.

(a) A principal may designate more than one attorney-in-fact in one or more powers of attorney.

(b) Authority granted to two or more attorneys-in-fact is exercisable only by their unanimous action.

(c) If a vacancy occurs, the remaining attorneys-in-fact may exercise the authority conferred as if they are the only attorneys-in-fact.

(d) If an attorney-in-fact is unavailable because of absence, illness, or other temporary incapacity, the other attorneys-in-fact may exercise the authority under the power of attorney as if they are the only attorneys-in-fact, where necessary to accomplish the purposes of the power of attorney or to avoid irreparable injury to the principal's interests.

(e) An attorney-in-fact is not liable for the actions of other attorneys-in-fact, unless the attorney-in-fact participates in, knowingly acquiesces in, or conceals a breach of fiduciary duty committed by another attorney-in-fact.

§ 4203. Successor attorneys-in-fact; exclusion; liability.

(a) A principal may designate one or more successor attorneys-in-fact to act if the authority of a predecessor attorney-in-fact terminates.

(b) The principal may grant authority to another person, designated by name, by office, or by function, including the initial and any successor attorneys-in-fact, to designate at any time one or more successor attorneys-in-fact. This subdivision does not apply to a durable power of attorney for health care under Part 4 (commencing with Section 4600).

(c) A successor attorney-in-fact is not liable for the actions of the predecessor attorney-in-fact.

§ 4204. Compensation.

An attorney-in-fact is entitled to reasonable compensation for services rendered to the principal as attorney-in-fact and to reimbursement for reasonable expenses incurred as a result of acting as attorney-in-fact.

§ 4205. Delegated authority.

(a) An attorney-in-fact may revocably delegate authority to perform mechanical acts to one or more persons qualified to exercise the authority delegated.

(b) The attorney-in-fact making a delegation remains responsible to the principal for the exercise or nonexercise of the delegated authority.

§ 4206. Court-appointed fiduciary; management of principal's property; accountability of attorney-in-fact; modification or revocation by conservator.

(a) If, following execution of a durable power of attorney, a court of the principal's domicile appoints a conservator of the estate, guardian of the estate, or other fiduciary charged with the management of all of the principal's property or all of the principal' s property except specified exclusions, the attorney-in-fact is accountable to the fiduciary as well as to the principal. Except as provided in subdivision (b), the fiduciary has the same power to revoke or amend the durable power of attorney that the principal would have had if not incapacitated, subject to any required court approval.

(b) If a conservator of the estate is appointed by a court of this state, the conservator can revoke or amend the durable power of attorney only if the court in which the conservatorship proceeding is pending has first made an order authorizing or requiring the fiduciary to modify or revoke the durable power of attorney and the modification or revocation is in accord with the order.

(c) This section does not apply to a durable power of attorney for health care.

(d) This section is not subject to limitation in the power of attorney.

§ 4207. Resignation.

(a) An attorney-in-fact may resign by any of the following means:

(1) If the principal is competent, by giving notice to the principal.

(2) If a conservator has been appointed, by giving notice to the conservator.

(3) On written agreement of a successor who is designated in the power of attorney or pursuant to the terms of the power of attorney to serve as attorney-in-fact.

(4) Pursuant to a court order.

(b) This section is not subject to limitation in the power of attorney.

SECTIONS 4230-4238

§ 4230. Duty to exercise authority; completing transaction; written agreements; consideration.

(a) Except as provided in subdivisions (b) and (c), a person who is designated as an attorney-in-fact has no duty to exercise the authority granted in the power of attorney and is not subject to the other duties of an attorney-in-fact, regardless of whether the principal has become incapacitated, is missing, or is otherwise unable to act.

(b) Acting for the principal in one or more transactions does not obligate an attorney-in-fact to act for the principal in a subsequent transaction, but the attorney-in-fact has a duty to complete a transaction that the attorney-in-fact has commenced.

(c) If an attorney-in-fact has expressly agreed in writing to act for the principal, the attorney-in-fact has a duty to act pursuant to the terms of the agreement. The agreement to act on behalf of the principal is enforceable against the attorney-in-fact as a fiduciary regardless of whether there is any consideration to support a contractual obligation.

§ 4231. Principal's property; standard of care; liability for loss; special skills or expertise.

(a) Except as provided in subdivisions (b) and (c), in dealing with property of the principal, an attorney-in-fact shall observe the standard of care that would be observed by a prudent person dealing with property of another and is not limited by any other statute restricting investments by fiduciaries.

(b) If an attorney-in-fact is not compensated, the attorney-in-fact is not liable for a loss to the principal's property unless the loss results from the attorney-in-fact's bad faith, intentional wrongdoing, or gross negligence.

(c) An attorney-in-fact who has special skills or expertise or was designated as an attorney-in-fact on the basis of representations of special skills or expertise shall observe the standard of care that would be observed by others with similar skills or expertise.

§ 4232. Principal's interests; conflicts.

(a) An attorney-in-fact has a duty to act solely in the interest of the principal and to avoid conflicts of interest.

(b) An attorney-in-fact is not in violation of the duty provided in subdivision (a) solely because the attorney-in-fact also benefits from acting for the principal, has conflicting interests in relation to the property, care, or affairs of the principal, or acts in an inconsistent manner regarding the respective interests of the principal and the attorney-in-fact.

§ 4233. Principal's property kept separate and distinct from other property.

(a) The attorney-in-fact shall keep the principal's property separate and distinct from other property in a manner adequate to identify the property clearly as belonging to the principal.

(b) An attorney-in-fact holding property for a principal complies with subdivision (a) if the property is held in the name of the principal or in the name of the attorney-in-fact as attorney-in-fact for the principal.

§ 4234. Regular contact and communication with principal; instruction; disobedience.

(a) To the extent reasonably practicable under the circumstances, an attorney-in-fact has a duty to keep in regular contact with the principal, to communicate with the principal, and to follow the instructions of the principal.

(b) With court approval, the attorney-in-fact may disobey instructions of the principal.

§ 4235. Principal's incapacity; consultation and disclosures from third persons; privileges.

If the principal becomes wholly or partially incapacitated, or if there is a question concerning the capacity of the principal to give instructions to and supervise the attorney-in-fact, the attorney-in-fact may consult with a person previously designated by the principal for this purpose, and may also consult with and obtain information needed to carry out the attorney-in-fact's duties from the principal's spouse, physician, attorney, accountant, a member of the principal's family, or other person, business entity, or government agency with respect to matters to be undertaken on the principal's behalf and affecting the principal's personal affairs, welfare, family, property, and business interests. A person from whom information is requested shall disclose relevant information to the attorney-in-fact. Disclosure under this section is not a waiver of any privilege that may apply to the information disclosed.

§ 4236. Records; account of transactions; examination of records.

(a) The attorney-in-fact shall keep records of all transactions entered into by the attorney-in-fact on behalf of the principal.

(b) The attorney-in-fact does not have a duty to make an account of transactions entered into on behalf of the principal, except in the following circumstances:

(1) At any time requested by the principal.

(2) Where the power of attorney requires the attorney-in-fact to account and specifies to whom the account is to be made.

(3) On request by the conservator of the estate of the principal while the principal is living.

(4) On request by the principal's personal representative or successor in interest after the death of the principal.

(5) Pursuant to court order.

(c) The following persons are entitled to examine and copy the records kept by the attorney-in-fact:

(1) The principal.

(2) The conservator of the estate of the principal while the principal is living.

(3) The principal's personal representative or successor in interest after the death of the principal.

(4) Any other person, pursuant to court order.

(d) This section is not subject to limitation in the power of attorney.

§ 4237. Special skills; standard of care.

An attorney-in-fact with special skills has a duty to apply the full extent of those skills.

§ 4238. Delivery of property upon termination of authority; records; accounting.

(a) On termination of an attorney-in-fact's authority, the attorney-in-fact shall promptly deliver possession or control of the principal's property as follows:

(1) If the principal is not incapacitated, to the principal or as directed by the principal.

(2) If the principal is incapacitated, to the following persons with the following priority:

(A) To a qualified successor attorney-in-fact.

(B) As to any community property, to the principal's spouse.

(C) To the principal's conservator of the estate or guardian of the estate.

(3) In the case of the death of the principal, to the principal's personal representative, if any, or the principal's successors.

(b) On termination of an attorney-in-fact's authority, the attorney-in-fact shall deliver copies of any records relating to transactions undertaken on the principal's behalf that are requested by the person to whom possession or control of the property is delivered.

(c) Termination of an attorney-in-fact's authority does not relieve the attorney-in-fact of any duty to render an account of actions taken as attorney-in-fact.

(d) The attorney-in-fact has the powers reasonably necessary under the circumstances to perform the duties provided by this section.

SECTIONS 4260-4266

§ 4260. Application of article.

This article does not apply to the following:

(a) Statutory form powers of attorney under Part 3 (commencing with Section 4400).

(b) Durable powers of attorney for health care under Part 4 (commencing with Section 4600).

§ 4261. General authority granted.

If a power of attorney grants general authority to an attorney-in-fact and is not limited to one or more express actions, subjects, or purposes for which general authority is conferred, the attorney-in-fact has all the authority to act that a person having the capacity to contract may carry out through an attorney-in-fact specifically authorized to take the action.

§ 4262. Limited authority granted.

Subject to this article, if a power of attorney grants limited authority to an attorney-in-fact, the attorney-in-fact has the following authority:

(a) The authority granted in the power of attorney, as limited with respect to permissible actions, subjects, or purposes.

(b) The authority incidental, necessary, or proper to carry out the granted authority.

§ 4263. Powers incorporated by reference to other statutes.

(a) A power of attorney may grant authority to the attorney-in-fact by incorporating powers by reference to another statute, including, but not limited to, the following:

(1) Powers of attorneys-in-fact provided by the Uniform Statutory Form Power of Attorney Act (Part 3 (commencing with Section 4400)).

(2) Powers of guardians and conservators provided by Chapter 5 (commencing with Section 2350) and Chapter 6 (commencing with Section 2400) of Part 4 of Division 4.

(3) Powers of trustees provided by Chapter 2 (commencing with Section 16200) of Part 4 of Division 9.

(b) Incorporation by reference to another statute includes any amendments made to the incorporated provisions after the date of execution of the power of attorney.

§ 4264. Acts requiring express authorization in power of attorney.

A power of attorney may not be construed to grant authority to an attorney-in-fact to perform any of the following acts unless expressly authorized in the power of attorney:

(a) Create, modify, or revoke a trust.

(b) Fund with the principal's property a trust not created by the principal or a person authorized to create a trust on behalf of the principal.

(c) Make or revoke a gift of the principal's property in trust or otherwise.

(d) Exercise the right to make a disclaimer on behalf of the principal. This subdivision does not limit the attorney-in-fact's authority to disclaim a detrimental transfer to the principal with the approval of the court.

(e) Create or change survivorship interests in the principal's property or in property in which the principal may have an interest.

(f) Designate or change the designation of beneficiaries to receive any property, benefit, or contract right on the principal's death.

(g) Make a loan to the attorney-in-fact.

§ 4265. Acts that power of attorney may not authorize.

A power of attorney may not authorize an attorney-in-fact to perform any of the following acts:

(a) Make, publish, declare, amend, or revoke the principal's will.

(b) Consent to any action under a durable power of attorney for health care forbidden by Section 4722.

§ 4266. Exercise of authority; fiduciary duties.

The grant of authority to an attorney-in-fact, whether by the power of attorney, by statute, or by the court, does not in itself require or permit the exercise of the power. The exercise of authority by an attorney-in-fact is subject to the attorney-in-fact's fiduciary duties.

SECTIONS 4300-4310

§ 4300. Rights and privileges of attorney-in-fact.

A third person shall accord an attorney-in-fact acting pursuant to the provisions of a power of attorney the same rights and privileges that would be accorded the principal if the principal were personally present and seeking to act. However, a third person is not required to honor the attorney-in-fact's authority or conduct business with the attorney-in-fact if the principal cannot require the third person to act or conduct business in the same circumstances.

§ 4301. Reliance on attorney-in-fact's acts, transactions or decisions.

A third person may rely on, contract with, and deal with an attorney-in-fact with respect to the subjects and purposes encompassed or expressed in the power of attorney without regard to whether the power of attorney expressly authorizes the specific act, transaction, or decision by the attorney-in-fact.

§ 4302. Identification, signature specimens and other information.

When requested to engage in transactions with an attorney-in-fact, a third person, before incurring any duty to comply with the power of attorney, may require the attorney-in-fact to provide identification, specimens of the signatures of the principal and the attorney-in-fact, and any other information reasonably necessary or appropriate to identify the principal and the attorney-in-fact and to facilitate the actions of the third person in transacting business with the attorney-in-fact. A third person may require an attorney-in-fact to provide the current and permanent residence addresses of the principal before agreeing to engage in a transaction with the attorney-in-fact.

§ 4303. Good faith reliance on power of attorney; third person's liability.

(a) A third person who acts in good faith reliance on a power of attorney is not liable to the principal or to any other person for so acting if all of the following requirements are satisfied:

(1) The power of attorney is presented to the third person by the attorney-in-fact designated in the power of attorney.

(2) The power of attorney appears on its face to be valid.

(3) The power of attorney includes a notary public's certificate of acknowledgment or is signed by two witnesses.

(b) Nothing in this section is intended to create an implication that a third person is liable for acting in reliance on a power of attorney under circumstances where the requirements of subdivision (a) are not satisfied. Nothing in this section affects any immunity that may otherwise exist apart from this section.

§ 4304. Death or incapacity of principal; knowledge; good faith acts.

(a) The death of a principal who has executed a power of attorney, whether durable or nondurable, does not revoke or terminate the agency as to the attorney-in-fact or a third person who, without actual knowledge of the principal's death, acts in good faith under the power of attorney. Any action so taken, unless otherwise invalid or unenforceable, binds the principal's successors in interest.

(b) The incapacity of a principal who has previously executed a nondurable power of attorney does not revoke or terminate the agency as to the attorney-in-fact or a third person who, without actual knowledge of the incapacity of the principal, acts in good faith under the power of attorney. Any action so taken, unless otherwise invalid or unenforceable, binds the principal and the principal's successors in interest.

§ 4305. Acts undertaken without knowledge of revoked power or principal's death or incapacity; affidavit; recordation.

(a) As to acts undertaken in good faith reliance thereon, an affidavit executed by the attorney-in-fact under a power of attorney, whether durable or nondurable, stating that, at the time of the exercise of the power, the attorney-in-fact did not have actual knowledge of the termination of the power of attorney or the attorney-in-fact's authority by revocation or of the principal's death or incapacity is conclusive proof of the nonrevocation or nontermination of the power at that time. If the exercise of the power of attorney requires execution and delivery of any instrument that is recordable, the affidavit when authenticated for record is likewise recordable.

(b) This section does not affect any provision in a power of attorney for its termination by expiration of time or occurrence of an event other than express revocation or a change in the principal's capacity.

§ 4306. Refusal to accept attorney-in-fact's authority referred to in affidavit; confirmation; attorney's fees; good faith actions.

(a) If an attorney-in-fact furnishes an affidavit pursuant to Section 4305, whether voluntarily or on demand, a third person dealing with the attorney-in-fact who refuses to accept the exercise of the attorney-in-fact's authority referred to in the affidavit is liable for attorney's fees incurred in an action or proceeding necessary to confirm the attorney-in-fact's qualifications or authority, unless the court determines that the third person believed in good faith that the attorney-in-fact was not qualified or was attempting to exceed or improperly exercise the attorney-in-fact's authority.

(b) The failure of a third person to demand an affidavit pursuant to Section 4305 does not affect the protection provided the third person by this chapter, and no inference as to whether a third person has acted in good faith may be drawn from the failure to demand an affidavit from the attorney-in-fact.

§ 4307. Certified copies of power of attorney.

(a) A copy of a power of attorney certified under this section has the same force and effect as the original power of attorney.

(b) A copy of a power of attorney may be certified by any of the following:

(1) An attorney authorized to practice law in this state.

(2) A notary public in this state.

(3) An official of a state or of a political subdivision who is authorized to make certifications.

(c) The certification shall state that the certifying person has examined the original power of attorney and the copy and that the copy is a true and correct copy of the original power of attorney.

(d) Nothing in this section is intended to create an implication that a third person may be liable for acting in good faith reliance on a copy of a power of attorney that has not been certified under this section.

§ 4308. Actual knowledge; third persons conducting activities through employees; branches or multiple offices.

(a) A third person who conducts activities through employees is not charged under this chapter with actual knowledge of any fact relating to a power of attorney, nor of a change in the authority of an attorney-in-fact, unless both of the following requirements are satisfied:

(1) The information is received at a home office or a place where there is an employee with responsibility to act on the information.

(2) The employee has a reasonable time in which to act on the information using the procedure and facilities that are available to the third person in the regular course of its operations.

(b) Knowledge of an employee in one branch or office of an entity that conducts business through branches or multiple offices is not attributable to an employee in another branch or office.

§ 4309. Agreements breached by attorney-in-fact; future transactions.

Nothing in this chapter requires a third person to engage in any transaction with an attorney-in-fact if the attorney-in-fact has previously breached any agreement with the third person.

§ 4310. Deposit accounts or loans at financial institutions; principal not currently a depositor or borrower.

Without limiting the generality of Section 4300, nothing in this chapter requires a financial institution to open a deposit account for a principal at the request of an attorney-in-fact if the principal is not currently a depositor of the financial institution or to make a loan to the attorney-in-fact on the principal's behalf if the principal is not currently a borrower of the financial institution.

SECTIONS 4400-4409

§ 4400. Short title.

This part may be cited as the Uniform Statutory Form Power of Attorney Act.

§ 4401. Form.

The following statutory form power of attorney is legally sufficient when the requirements of Section 4402 are satisfied:

[See Form A in appendix B
and Form 1 in appendix C]

§ 4402. Legal sufficiency of form; conditions.

A statutory form power of attorney under this part is legally sufficient if all of the following requirements are satisfied:

(a) The wording of the form complies substantially with Section 4401. A form does not fail to comply substantially with Section 4401 merely because the form does not include the provisions of Section 4401 relating to designation of co-agents. A form does not fail to comply substantially with Section 4401 merely because the form uses the sentence "Revocation of the power of attorney is not effective as to a third party until the third party learns of the revocation" in place of the sentence "Revocation of the power of attorney is not effective as to a third party until the third party has actual knowledge of the revocation," in which case the form shall be interpreted as if it contained the sentence "Revocation of the power of attorney is not effective as to a third party until the third party has actual knowledge of the revocation."

(b) The form is properly completed.

(c) The signature of the principal is acknowledged.

§ 4403. Initialed lines on form; limitation of powers.

If the line in front of (N) of the statutory form under Section 4401 is initialed, an initial on the line in front of any other power does not limit the powers granted by line (N).

§ 4404. Durable power of attorney; language showing principal's intent.

A statutory form power of attorney legally sufficient under this part is durable to the extent that the power of attorney contains language, such as "This power of attorney will continue to be effective even though I become incapacitated," showing the intent of the principal that the power granted may be exercised notwithstanding later incapacity.

§ 4405. Power dependent on occurrence of event or contingency; determination that event has occurred; written declaration; liability.

(a) A statutory form power of attorney under this part that limits the power to take effect upon the occurrence of a specified event or contingency, including, but not limited to, the incapacity of the principal, may contain a provision designating one or more persons who, by a written declaration under penalty of perjury, have the power to determine conclusively that the specified event or contingency has occurred.

(b) A statutory form power of attorney that contains the provision described in subdivision (a) becomes effective when the person or persons designated in the power of attorney execute a written declaration under penalty of perjury that the specified event or contingency has occurred, and any person may act in reliance on the written declaration without liability to the principal or to any other person, regardless whether the specified event or contingency has actually occurred.

(c) The provision described in subdivision (a) may be included in the "Special Instructions" portion of the form set forth in Section 4401.

(d) Subdivisions (a) and (b) do not provide the exclusive method by which a statutory form power of attorney under this part may be limited to take effect upon the occurrence of a specified event or contingency.

§ 4406. Third person's refusal to honor agent's authority under power of attorney; action to compel honor; remedies.

(a) If a third person to whom a properly executed statutory form power of attorney under this part is presented refuses to honor the agent's authority under the power of attorney within a reasonable time, the third person may be compelled to honor the agent's authority under the power of attorney in an action brought against the third person for this purpose, except that the third person may not be compelled to honor the agent's authority if the principal could not compel the third person to act in the same circumstances.

(b) If an action is brought under this section, the court shall award attorney's fees to the agent if the court finds that the third person acted unreasonably in refusing to accept the agent's authority under the statutory form power of attorney.

(c) For the purpose of subdivision (b), and without limiting any other grounds that may constitute a reasonable refusal to accept an agent's authority under a statutory form power of attorney, a third person shall not be deemed to have acted unreasonably in refusing to accept an agent's authority if the refusal is authorized or required by state or federal statute or regulation.

(d) Notwithstanding subdivision (c), a third person's refusal to accept an agent's authority under a statutory form power of attorney under this part shall be deemed unreasonable if the only reason for the refusal is that the power of attorney is not on a form prescribed by the third person to whom the power of attorney is presented.

(e) The remedy provided in this section is cumulative and nonexclusive.

§ 4407. Application of division to statutory form power of attorney; conflicting provisions.

Unless there is a conflicting provision in this part, in which case the provision of this part governs, the other provisions of this division apply to a statutory form power of attorney.

§ 4408. Other forms; application of this part.

Nothing in this part affects or limits the use of any other form for a power of attorney. A form that complies with the requirements of any law other than the provisions of this part may be used instead of the form set forth in Section 4401, and none of the provisions of this part apply if the other form is used.

§ 4409. Statutory short form powers of attorney executed under prior law; validity.

(a) A statutory short form power of attorney executed before, on, or after the repeal of Chapter 3 (commencing with Section 2450) of Title 9 of Part 4 of Division 3 of the Civil Code by Chapter 986 of the Statutes of 1990, using a form that complied with former Section 2450 of the Civil Code, as originally enacted by Chapter 602 of the Statutes of 1984, or as amended by Chapter 403 of the Statutes of 1985, is as valid as if Chapter 3 (commencing with Section 2450) of Title 9 of Part 4 of Division 3 of the Civil Code had not been repealed by, and former Section 2511 of the Civil Code amended by, Chapter 986 of the Statutes of 1990.

(b) A statutory form power of attorney executed before, on, or after the repeal of Chapter 3.5 (commencing with Section 2475) of Title 9 of Part 4 of Division 3 of the Civil Code by the act that enacted this section, using a form that complied with the repealed chapter of the Civil Code is as valid as if that chapter had not been repealed.

SECTIONS 4450-4465

§ 4450. Subjects covered by statutory form power of attorney; general powers.

By executing a statutory form power of attorney with respect to a subject listed in Section 4401, the principal, except as limited or extended by the principal in the power of attorney, empowers the agent, for that subject, to do all of the following:

(a) Demand, receive, and obtain by litigation or otherwise, money or other thing of value to which the principal is, may become, or claims to be entitled, and conserve, invest, disburse, or use anything so received for the purposes intended.

(b) Contract in any manner with any person, on terms agreeable to the agent, to accomplish a purpose of a transaction, and perform, rescind, reform, release, or modify the contract or another contract made by or on behalf of the principal.

(c) Execute, acknowledge, seal, and deliver a deed, revocation, mortgage, lease, notice, check, release, or other instrument the agent considers desirable to accomplish a purpose of a transaction.

(d) Prosecute, defend, submit to arbitration, settle, and propose or accept a compromise with respect to, a claim existing in favor of or against the principal or intervene in litigation relating to the claim.

(e) Seek on the principal's behalf the assistance of a court to carry out an act authorized by the power of attorney.

(f) Engage, compensate, and discharge an attorney, accountant, expert witness, or other assistant.

(g) Keep appropriate records of each transaction, including an accounting of receipts and disbursements.

(h) Prepare, execute, and file a record, report, or other document the agent considers desirable to safeguard or promote the principal' s interest under a statute or governmental regulation.

(i) Reimburse the agent for expenditures properly made by the agent in exercising the powers granted by the power of attorney.

(j) In general, do any other lawful act with respect to the subject.

§ 4451. Real property transactions; powers granted.

In a statutory form power of attorney, the language granting power with respect to real property transactions empowers the agent to do all of the following:

(a) Accept as a gift or as security for a loan, reject, demand, buy, lease, receive, or otherwise acquire, an interest in real property or a right incident to real property.

(b) Sell, exchange, convey with or without covenants, quitclaim, release, surrender, mortgage, encumber, partition, consent to partitioning, subdivide, apply for zoning, rezoning, or other governmental permits, plat or consent to platting, develop, grant options concerning, lease, sublease, or otherwise dispose of, an interest in real property or a right incident to real property.

(c) Release, assign, satisfy, and enforce by litigation or otherwise, a mortgage, deed of trust, encumbrance, lien, or other claim to real property which exists or is asserted.

(d) Do any act of management or of conservation with respect to an interest in real property, or a right incident to real property, owned, or claimed to be owned, by the principal, including all of the following:

(1) Insuring against a casualty, liability, or loss.

(2) Obtaining or regaining possession, or protecting the interest or right, by litigation or otherwise.

(3) Paying, compromising, or contesting taxes or assessments, or applying for and receiving refunds in connection with them.

(4) Purchasing supplies, hiring assistance or labor, and making repairs or alterations in the real property.

(e) Use, develop, alter, replace, remove, erect, or install structures or other improvements upon real property in or incident to which the principal has, or claims to have, an interest or right.

(f) Participate in a reorganization with respect to real property or a legal entity that owns an interest in or right incident to real property and receive and hold shares of stock or obligations received in a plan of reorganization, and act with respect to them, including all of the following:

(1) Selling or otherwise disposing of them.

(2) Exercising or selling an option, conversion, or similar right with respect to them.

(3) Voting them in person or by proxy.

(g) Change the form of title of an interest in or right incident to real property.

(h) Dedicate to public use, with or without consideration, easements or other real property in which the principal has, or claims to have, an interest or right.

§ 4452. Tangible personal property transactions; powers granted.

In a statutory form power of attorney, the language granting power with respect to tangible personal property transactions empowers the agent to do all of the following:

(a) Accept as a gift or as security for a loan, reject, demand, buy, receive, or otherwise acquire ownership or possession of tangible personal property or an interest in tangible personal property.

(b) Sell, exchange, convey with or without covenants, release, surrender, mortgage, encumber, pledge, hypothecate, create a security interest in, pawn, grant options concerning, lease, sublease to others, or otherwise dispose of tangible personal property or an interest in tangible personal property.

(c) Release, assign, satisfy, or enforce by litigation or otherwise, a mortgage, security interest, encumbrance, lien, or other claim on behalf of the principal, with respect to tangible personal property or an interest in tangible personal property.

(d) Do an act of management or conservation with respect to tangible personal property or an interest in tangible personal property on behalf of the principal, including all of the following:

(1) Insuring against casualty, liability, or loss.

(2) Obtaining or regaining possession, or protecting the property or interest, by litigation or otherwise.

(3) Paying, compromising, or contesting taxes or assessments or applying for and receiving refunds in connection with taxes or assessments.

(4) Moving from place to place.

(5) Storing for hire or on a gratuitous bailment.

(6) Using, altering, and making repairs or alterations.

§ 4453. Stock and bond transactions; powers granted.

In a statutory form power of attorney, the language granting power with respect to stock and bond transactions empowers the agent to do all of the following:

(a) Buy, sell, and exchange stocks, bonds, mutual funds, and all other types of securities and financial instruments except commodity futures contracts and call and put options on stocks and stock indexes.

(b) Receive certificates and other evidences of ownership with respect to securities.

(c) Exercise voting rights with respect to securities in person or by proxy, enter into voting trusts, and consent to limitations on the right to vote.

§ 4454. Commodity and option transactions; powers granted.

In a statutory form power of attorney, the language granting power with respect to commodity and option transactions empowers the agent to do all of the following:

(a) Buy, sell, exchange, assign, settle, and exercise commodity futures contracts and call and put options on stocks and stock indexes traded on a regulated option exchange.

(b) Establish, continue, modify, and terminate option accounts with a broker.

§ 4455. Banking and other financial institution transactions; powers granted.

In a statutory form power of attorney, the language granting power with respect to banking and other financial institution transactions empowers the agent to do all of the following:

(a) Continue, modify, and terminate an account or other banking arrangement made by or on behalf of the principal.

(b) Establish, modify, and terminate an account or other banking arrangement with a bank, trust company, savings and loan association, credit union, thrift company, industrial loan company, brokerage firm, or other financial institution selected by the agent.

(c) Hire or close a safe deposit box or space in a vault.

(d) Contract to procure other services available from a financial institution as the agent considers desirable.

(e) Withdraw by check, order, or otherwise money or property of the principal deposited with or left in the custody of a financial institution.

(f) Receive bank statements, vouchers, notices, and similar documents from a financial institution and act with respect to them.

(g) Enter a safe deposit box or vault and withdraw or add to the contents.

(h) Borrow money at an interest rate agreeable to the agent and pledge as security personal property of the principal necessary in order to borrow, pay, renew, or extend the time of payment of a debt of the principal.

(i) Make, assign, draw, endorse, discount, guarantee, and negotiate promissory notes, checks, drafts, and other negotiable or nonnegotiable paper of the principal, or payable to the principal or the principal's order, receive the cash or other proceeds of those transactions, and accept a draft drawn by a person upon the principal and pay it when due.

(j) Receive for the principal and act upon a sight draft, warehouse receipt, or other negotiable or nonnegotiable instrument.

(k) Apply for and receive letters of credit, credit cards, and traveler's checks from a financial institution, and give an indemnity or other agreement in connection with letters of credit.

(l) Consent to an extension of the time of payment with respect to commercial paper or a financial transaction with a financial institution.

§ 4456. Business operating transactions; powers granted.

In a statutory form power of attorney, the language granting power with respect to business operating transactions empowers the agent to do all of the following:

(a) Operate, buy, sell, enlarge, reduce, and terminate a business interest.

(b) To the extent that an agent is permitted by law to act for a principal and subject to the terms of the partnership agreement:

(1) Perform a duty or discharge a liability and exercise a right, power, privilege, or option that the principal has, may have, or claims to have, under a partnership agreement, whether or not the principal is a partner.

(2) Enforce the terms of a partnership agreement by litigation or otherwise.

(3) Defend, submit to arbitration, settle, or compromise litigation to which the principal is a party because of membership in the partnership.

(c) Exercise in person or by proxy, or enforce by litigation or otherwise, a right, power, privilege, or option the principal has or claims to have as the holder of a bond, share, or other instrument of similar character, and defend, submit to arbitration, settle, or compromise litigation to which the principal is a party because of a bond, share, or similar instrument.

(d) With respect to a business owned solely by the principal:

(1) Continue, modify, renegotiate, extend, and terminate a contract made with an individual or a legal entity, firm, association, or corporation by or on behalf of the principal with respect to the business before execution of the power of attorney.

(2) Determine the policy of the business as to (A) the location of its operation, (B) the nature and extent of its business, (C) the methods of manufacturing, selling, merchandising, financing, accounting, and advertising employed in its operation, (D) the amount and types of insurance carried, and (E) the mode of engaging, compensating, and dealing with its accountants, attorneys, and other agents and employees.

(3) Change the name or form of organization under which the business is operated and enter into a partnership agreement with other persons or organize a corporation to take over all or part of the operation of the business.

(4) Demand and receive money due or claimed by the principal or on the principal's behalf in the operation of the business, and control and disburse the money in the operation of the business.

(e) Put additional capital into a business in which the principal has an interest.

(f) Join in a plan of reorganization, consolidation, or merger of the business.

(g) Sell or liquidate a business or part of it at the time and upon the terms the agent considers desirable.

(h) Represent the principal in establishing the value of a business under a buy-out agreement to which the principal is a party.

(i) Prepare, sign, file, and deliver reports, compilations of information, returns, or other papers with respect to a business which are required by a governmental agency or instrumentality or which the agent considers desirable, and make related payments.

(j) Pay, compromise, or contest taxes or assessments and do any other act which the agent considers desirable to protect the principal from illegal or unnecessary taxation, fines, penalties, or assessments with respect to a business, including attempts to recover, in any manner permitted by law, money paid before or after the execution of the power of attorney.

§ 4457. Insurance and annuity transactions; powers granted.

In a statutory form power of attorney, the language granting power with respect to insurance and annuity transactions empowers the agent to do all of the following:

(a) Continue, pay the premium or assessment on, modify, rescind, release, or terminate a contract procured by or on behalf of the principal which insures or provides an annuity to either the principal or another person, whether or not the principal is a beneficiary under the contract.

(b) Procure new, different, and additional contracts of insurance and annuities for the principal and the principal's spouse, children, and other dependents, and select the amount, type of insurance or annuity, and mode of payment.

(c) Pay the premium or assessment on, modify, rescind, release, or terminate a contract of insurance or annuity procured by the agent.

(d) Designate the beneficiary of the contract, but the agent may be named a beneficiary of the contract, or an extension, renewal, or substitute for it, only to the extent the agent was named as a beneficiary under a contract procured by the principal before executing the power of attorney.

(e) Apply for and receive a loan on the security of the contract of insurance or annuity.

(f) Surrender and receive the cash surrender value.

(g) Exercise an election.

(h) Change the manner of paying premiums.

(i) Change or convert the type of insurance contract or annuity as to any insurance contract or annuity with respect to which the principal has or claims to have a power described in this section.

(j) Change the beneficiary of a contract of insurance or annuity, but the agent may not be designated a beneficiary except to the extent permitted by subdivision (d).

(k) Apply for and procure government aid to guarantee or pay premiums of a contract of insurance on the life of the principal.

(l) Collect, sell, assign, hypothecate, borrow upon, or pledge the interest of the principal in a contract of insurance or annuity.

(m) Pay from proceeds or otherwise, compromise or contest, and apply for refunds in connection with, a tax or assessment levied by a taxing authority with respect to a contract of insurance or annuity or its proceeds or liability accruing by reason of the tax or assessment.

§ 4458. Estate, trust and other beneficiary transactions; powers granted.

In a statutory form power of attorney, the language granting power with respect to estate, trust, and other beneficiary transactions, empowers the agent to act for the principal in all matters that affect a trust, probate estate, guardianship, conservatorship, escrow, custodianship, or other fund from which the principal is, may become, or claims to be entitled, as a beneficiary, to a share or payment, including the power to do all of the following:

(a) Accept, reject, disclaim, receive, receipt for, sell, assign, release, pledge, exchange, or consent to a reduction in or modification of a share in or payment from the fund.

(b) Demand or obtain by litigation or otherwise money or other thing of value to which the principal is, may become, or claims to be entitled by reason of the fund.

(c) Initiate, participate in, and oppose litigation to ascertain the meaning, validity, or effect of a deed, will, declaration of trust, or other instrument or transaction affecting the interest of the principal.

(d) Initiate, participate in, and oppose litigation to remove, substitute, or surcharge a fiduciary.

(e) Conserve, invest, disburse, and use anything received for an authorized purpose.

(f) Transfer an interest of the principal in real property, stocks, bonds, accounts with financial institutions, insurance, and other property, to the trustee of a revocable trust created by the principal as settlor.

§ 4459. Claims and litigation; powers granted.

In a statutory form power of attorney, the language with respect to claims and litigation empowers the agent to do all of the following:

(a) Assert and prosecute before a court or administrative agency a claim, claim for relief, cause of action, counterclaim, cross-complaint, or offset, and defend against an individual, a legal entity, or government, including suits to recover property or other thing of value, to recover damages sustained by the principal, to eliminate or modify tax liability, or to seek an injunction, specific performance, or other relief.

(b) Bring an action to determine adverse claims, intervene in litigation, and act as amicus curiae.

(c) In connection with litigation:

(1) Procure an attachment, garnishment, libel, order of arrest, or other preliminary, provisional, or intermediate relief and use any available procedure to effect, enforce, or satisfy a judgment, order, or decree.

(2) Perform any lawful act, including acceptance of tender, offer of judgment, admission of facts, submission of a controversy on an agreed statement of facts, consent to examination before trial, and binding the principal in litigation.

(d) Submit to arbitration, settle, and propose or accept a compromise with respect to a claim or litigation.

(e) Waive the issuance and service of process upon the principal, accept service of process, appear for the principal, designate persons upon whom process directed to the principal may be served, execute and file or deliver stipulations on the principal's behalf, verify pleadings, seek appellate review, procure and give surety and indemnity bonds, contract and pay for the preparation and printing of records and briefs, receive and execute and file or deliver a consent, waiver, release, confession of judgment, satisfaction of judgment, notice, agreement, or other instrument in connection with the prosecution, settlement, or defense of a claim or litigation.

(f) Act for the principal with respect to bankruptcy or insolvency proceedings, whether voluntary or involuntary, concerning the principal or some other person, or with respect to a reorganization proceeding, or with respect to an assignment for the benefit of creditors, receivership, or application for the appointment of a receiver or trustee which affects an interest of the principal in property or other thing of value.

(g) Pay a judgment against the principal or a settlement made in connection with litigation and receive and conserve money or other thing of value paid in settlement of or as proceeds of a claim or litigation.

§ 4460. Personal and family maintenance; powers granted.

In a statutory form power of attorney, the language granting power with respect to personal and family maintenance empowers the agent to do all of the following:

(a) Do the acts necessary to maintain the customary standard of living of the principal, the principal's spouse, children, and other individuals customarily or legally entitled to be supported by the principal, including providing living quarters by purchase, lease, or other contract, or paying the operating costs, including interest, amortization payments, repairs, and taxes on premises owned by the principal and occupied by those individuals.

(b) Provide for the individuals described in subdivision (a) all of the following:

(1) Normal domestic help.

(2) Usual vacations and travel expenses.

(3) Funds for shelter, clothing, food, appropriate education, and other current living costs.

(c) Pay for the individuals described in subdivision (a) necessary medical, dental, and surgical care, hospitalization, and custodial care.

(d) Continue any provision made by the principal, for the individuals described in subdivision (a), for automobiles or other means of transportation, including registering, licensing, insuring, and replacing them.

(e) Maintain or open charge accounts for the convenience of the individuals described in subdivision (a) and open new accounts the agent considers desirable to accomplish a lawful purpose.

(f) Continue payments incidental to the membership or affiliation of the principal in a church, club, society, order, or other organization and continue contributions to those organizations.

§ 4461. Social security or other governmental program; civil or military benefit; powers granted.

In a statutory form power of attorney, the language granting power with respect to benefits from social security, medicare, medicaid, or other governmental programs, or civil or military service, empowers the agent to do all of the following:

(a) Execute vouchers in the name of the principal for allowances and reimbursements payable by the United States or a foreign government or by a state or subdivision of a state to the principal, including allowances and reimbursements for transportation of the individuals described in subdivision (a) of Section 4460, and for shipment of their household effects.

(b) Take possession and order the removal and shipment of property of the principal from a post, warehouse, depot, dock, or other place of storage or safekeeping, either governmental or private, and execute and deliver a release, voucher, receipt, bill of lading, shipping ticket, certificate, or other instrument for that purpose.

(c) Prepare, file, and prosecute a claim of the principal to a benefit or assistance, financial or otherwise, to which the principal claims to be entitled, under a statute or governmental regulation.

(d) Prosecute, defend, submit to arbitration, settle, and propose or accept a compromise with respect to any benefits the principal may be entitled to receive.

(e) Receive the financial proceeds of a claim of the type described in this section, conserve, invest, disburse, or use anything received for a lawful purpose.

§ 4462. Retirement plan transactions; powers granted.

In a statutory form power of attorney, the language granting power with respect to retirement plan transactions empowers the agent to do all of the following:

(a) Select payment options under any retirement plan in which the principal participates, including plans for self-employed individuals.

(b) Designate beneficiaries under those plans and change existing designations.

(c) Make voluntary contributions to those plans.

(d) Exercise the investment powers available under any self-directed retirement plan.

(e) Make rollovers of plan benefits into other retirement plans.

(f) If authorized by the plan, borrow from, sell assets to, and purchase assets from the plan.

(g) Waive the right of the principal to be a beneficiary of a joint or survivor annuity if the principal is a spouse who is not employed.

§ 4463. Tax matters; powers granted.

In a statutory form power of attorney, the language granting power with respect to tax matters empowers the agent to do all of the following:

(a) Prepare, sign, and file federal, state, local, and foreign income, gift, payroll, Federal Insurance Contributions Act returns, and other tax returns, claims for refunds, requests for extension of time, petitions regarding tax matters, and any other tax-related documents, including receipts, offers, waivers, consents (including consents and agreements under Internal Revenue Code Section 2032A or any successor section), closing agreements, and any power of attorney required by the Internal Revenue Service or other taxing authority with respect to a tax year upon which the statute of limitations has not run and to the tax year in which the power of attorney was executed and any subsequent tax year.

(b) Pay taxes due, collect refunds, post bonds, receive confidential information, and contest deficiencies determined by the Internal Revenue Service or other taxing authority.

(c) Exercise any election available to the principal under federal, state, local, or foreign tax law.

(d) Act for the principal in all tax matters for all periods before the Internal Revenue Service and any other taxing authority.

§ 4464. After-acquired property; state where property is located or where power is executed.

The powers described in this chapter are exercisable equally with respect to an interest the principal has when the statutory form power of attorney is executed or acquires later, whether or not the property is located in this state, and whether or not the powers are exercised or the power of attorney is executed in this state.

§ 4465. Trusts; power to modify or revoke.

A statutory form power of attorney under this part does not empower the agent to modify or revoke a trust created by the principal unless that power is expressly granted by the power of attorney. If a statutory form power of attorney under this part empowers the agent to modify or revoke a trust created by the principal, the trust may only be modified or revoked by the agent as provided in the trust instrument.

SECTIONS 4600-4621

§ 4600. Definitions governing construction of part.

Unless the provision or context otherwise requires, the definitions in this article govern the construction of this part.

§ 4603. Community care facility.

"Community care facility" means a community care facility as defined in Section 1502 of the Health and Safety Code.

§ 4606. Durable power of attorney for health care.

"Durable power of attorney for health care" means a durable power of attorney to the extent that it authorizes an attorney-in-fact to make health care decisions for the principal.

§ 4609. Health care.

"Health care" means any care, treatment, service, or procedure to maintain, diagnose, or treat an individual's physical or mental condition and includes decisions affecting the principal after death.

§ 4612. Health care decision.

"Health care decision" means consent, refusal of consent, or withdrawal of consent to health care, or a decision to begin, continue, increase, limit, discontinue, or not to begin any health care.

§ 4615. Health care provider.

"Health care provider" means a person who is licensed, certified, or otherwise authorized or permitted by the law of this state to administer health care in the ordinary course of business or practice of a profession.

§ 4618. Residential care facility for the elderly.

"Residential care facility for the elderly" means a residential care facility for the elderly as defined in Section 1569.2 of the Health and Safety Code.

§ 4621. Statutory form durable power of attorney for health care

"Statutory form durable power of attorney for health care" means a durable power of attorney for health care that satisfies the requirements of Chapter 3 (commencing with Section 4770).

SECTION 4650-4654

§ 4650. Execution date of durable power of attorney; compliance with chapter; validity.

(a) A durable power of attorney executed on or after January 1, 1984, is effective to authorize the attorney-in-fact to make health care decisions for the principal only if the durable power of attorney complies with this chapter.

(b) A durable power of attorney executed before January 1, 1984, that specifically authorizes the attorney-in-fact to make decisions relating to the medical or health care of the principal shall be deemed to be valid under this chapter after January 1, 1984, notwithstanding that it fails to comply with subdivision (a) or (c) of Section 4121 or subdivision (a) of Section 4704; but, to the extent that the durable power of attorney authorizes the attorney-in-fact to make health care decisions for the principal, the durable power of attorney is subject to all the provisions of this chapter and to Part 5 (commencing with Section 4900).

(c) Nothing in this chapter affects the validity of a decision made under a durable power of attorney before January 1, 1984.

§ 4651. Sale or distribution of printed forms; date of printing; compliance with other statutes; advice of legal counsel; execution date.

(a) Notwithstanding Section 4703, on and after January 1, 1986, a printed form of a durable power of attorney for health care may be sold or otherwise distributed if it complies with former Section 2433 of the Civil Code as amended by Section 5 of Chapter 312 of the Statutes of 1984, or with former Section 2433 of the Civil Code as in effect at the time of sale or distribution. However, any printed form of a durable power of attorney for health care printed on or after January 1, 1986, that is sold or otherwise distributed in this state for use by a person who does not have the advice of legal counsel shall comply with former Section 2433 of the Civil Code or Section 4703 of this code in effect at the time of printing.

(b) Notwithstanding Section 4700, a printed form of a durable power of attorney for health care may be sold or otherwise distributed if it complies with former Section 2432 of the Civil Code as enacted by Section 10 of Chapter 1204 of the Statutes of 1983 or as subsequently amended, or with Section 4700 of this code. However, any printed form of a durable power of attorney for health care printed on or after January 1, 1986, shall comply with the requirements of former Section 2432 of the Civil Code or Section 4700 of this code in effect at the time of printing.

(c) A durable power of attorney for health care executed on or after January 1, 1986, is not invalid if it complies with former Section 2432 of the Civil Code as originally enacted or as subsequently amended. A durable power of attorney for health care executed on or after January 1, 1986, using a printed form that complied with former Section 2433 of the Civil Code, as amended by Section 5 of Chapter 312 of the Statutes of 1984, is as valid as if it had been executed using a printed form that complied with former Section 2433 of the Civil Code as thereafter amended or with Section 4703 of this code.

§ 4652. Health care decisions on behalf of another; emergency treatment.

(a) Subject to Sections 4720 and 4946, nothing in this part affects any right a person may have to make health care decisions on behalf of another if the attorney-in-fact and any successor attorney-in-fact are unavailable, unwilling, or unable to make health care decisions on behalf of the principal.

(b) This part does not affect the law governing health care treatment in an emergency.

§ 4653. Execution in another state; validity.

A durable power of attorney for health care or similar instrument executed in another state or jurisdiction in compliance with the laws of that state or jurisdiction or of this state, shall be valid and enforceable in this state to the same extent as a durable power of attorney for health care validly executed in this state.

§ 4654. Expiration of certain durable power of attorney for health care.

(a) This section applies only to a durable power of attorney for health care that satisfies one of the following requirements:

(1) The power of attorney was executed after January 1, 1984, but before January 1, 1992.

(2) The power of attorney was executed on or after January 1, 1992, and contains a warning statement that refers to a seven-year limit on its duration.

(b) Unless a shorter period is provided in the durable power of attorney for health care, a durable power of attorney for health care described in subdivision (a) expires seven years after the date of its execution unless at the end of the seven-year period the principal lacks the capacity to make health care decisions for himself or herself, in which case the durable power of attorney for health care continues in effect until the time when the principal regains the capacity to make health care decisions for himself or herself.

SECTIONS 4700-4704

§ 4700. Health care decisions by attorney-in-fact; conditions.

An attorney-in-fact under a durable power of attorney may not make health care decisions unless the durable power of attorney satisfies all of the following requirements:

(a) The power of attorney specifically grants authority to the attorney-in-fact to make health care decisions.

(b) The power of attorney is executed as provided in Section 4121.

(c) The power of attorney satisfies the requirements of this article.

§ 4701. Witnesses; declarations; eligibility.

If the durable power of attorney for health care is signed by witnesses, as provided in Section 4121, in addition to the requirements applicable to witnesses under Section 4122, the following requirements shall be satisfied:

(a) None of the following persons may act as a witness:

(1) The principal's health care provider or an employee of the principal's health care provider.

(2) The operator or an employee of a community care facility.

(3) The operator or an employee of a residential care facility for the elderly.

(b) Each witness shall make the following declaration in substance:

"I declare under penalty of perjury under the laws of California that the person who signed or acknowledged this document is personally known to me to be the principal, or that the identity of the principal was proved to me by convincing evidence, that the principal signed or acknowledged this durable power of attorney in my presence, that the principal appears to be of sound mind and under no duress, fraud, or undue influence, that I am not the person appointed as attorney-in-fact by this document, and that I am not the principal's health care provider, an employee of the principal's health care provider, the operator of a community care facility, an employee of an operator of a community care facility, the operator of a residential care facility for the elderly, nor an employee of an operator of a residential care facility for the elderly."

(c) At least one of the witnesses shall be a person who is not one of the following:

(1) A relative of the principal by blood, marriage, or adoption.

(2) A person who would be entitled to any portion of the principal' s estate upon the principal's death under a will existing at the time of execution of the durable power of attorney for health care or by operation of law then existing.

(d) The witness satisfying the requirement of subdivision (c) shall also sign the following declaration in substance:

"I further declare under penalty of perjury under the laws of California that I am not related to the principal by blood, marriage, or adoption, and, to the best of my knowledge, I am not entitled to any part of the principal's estate upon the principal's death under a will now existing or by operation of law."

(e) If the principal is a patient in a skilled nursing facility, as defined in subdivision (c) of Section 1250 of the Health and Safety Code, at the time the durable power of attorney for health care is executed, the power of attorney is not effective unless a patient advocate or ombudsman as may be designated by the Department of Aging for this purpose pursuant to any other applicable provision of law signs the instrument as a witness, either as one of two witnesses or in addition to notarization pursuant to subdivision

(c) of Section 4121. The patient advocate or ombudsman shall declare that he or she is serving as a witness as required by this subdivision. It is the intent of this subdivision to recognize that some patients in skilled nursing facilities are insulated from a voluntary decisionmaking role, by virtue of the custodial nature of their care, so as to require special assurance that they are capable of willfully and voluntarily executing a durable power of attorney for health care.

§ 4702. Attorney-in-fact to make health care decisions; permitted designees.

(a) Except as provided in subdivision (b), the following persons may not exercise authority to make health care decisions under a durable power of attorney:

(1) The treating health care provider or an employee of the treating health care provider.

(2) An operator or employee of a community care facility.

(3) An operator or employee of a residential care facility for the elderly.

(b) An employee of the treating health care provider or an employee of an operator of a community care facility or an employee of a residential care facility for the elderly may be designated as the attorney-in-fact to make health care decisions under a durable power of attorney for health care if both of the following requirements are met:

(1) The employee is a relative of the principal by blood, marriage, or adoption, or the employee is employed by the same treating health care provider, community care facility, or residential care facility for the elderly that employs the principal.

(2) The other requirements of this chapter are satisfied.

(c) Except as provided in subdivision (b), if a health care provider becomes the principal's treating health care provider, the health care provider or an employee of the health care provider may not exercise authority to make health care decisions under a durable power of attorney.

(d) A conservator may not be designated as the attorney-in-fact to make health care decisions under a durable power of attorney for health care executed by a person who is a conservatee under the Lanterman-Petris-Short Act (Part 1 (commencing with Section 5000) of Division 5 of the Welfare and Institutions Code), unless all of the following are satisfied:

(1) The power of attorney is otherwise valid.

(2) The conservatee is represented by legal counsel.

(3) The lawyer representing the conservatee signs a certificate stating in substance:

"I am a lawyer authorized to practice law in the state where this power of attorney was executed, and the principal was my client at the time this power of attorney was executed. I have advised my client concerning his or her rights in connection with this power of attorney and the applicable law and the consequences of signing or not signing this power of attorney, and my client, after being so advised, has executed this power of attorney."

§ 4703. Warning statement to person executing document; form.

(a) A printed form of a durable power of attorney for health care that is sold or otherwise distributed in this state for use by a person who does not have the advice of legal counsel shall provide no other authority than the authority to make health care decisions on behalf of the principal and shall contain, in not less than 10-point boldface type or a reasonable equivalent thereof, the following warning statement:

WARNING TO PERSON EXECUTING

THIS DOCUMENT

This is an important legal document. Before executing this document, you should know these important facts:

This document gives the person you designate as your agent (the attorney-in-fact) the power to make health care decisions for you. Your agent must act consistently with your desires as stated in this document or otherwise made known.

Except as you otherwise specify in this document, this document gives your agent the power to consent to your doctor not giving treatment or stopping treatment necessary to keep you alive.

Notwithstanding this document, you have the right to make medical and other health care decisions for yourself so long as you can give informed consent with respect to the particular decision. In addition, no treatment may be given to you over your objection, and health care necessary to keep you alive may not be stopped or withheld if you object at the time.

This document gives your agent authority to consent, to refuse to consent, or to withdraw consent to any care, treatment, service, or procedure to maintain, diagnose, or treat a physical or mental condition. This power is subject to any statement of your desires and any limitations that you include in this document. You may state in this document any types of treatment that you do not desire. In addition, a court can take away the power of your agent to make health care decisions for you if your agent (1) authorizes anything that is illegal, (2) acts contrary to your known desires, or (3) where your desires are not known, does anything that is clearly contrary to your best interests.

This power will exist for an indefinite period of time unless you limit its duration in this document.

You have the right to revoke the authority of your agent by notifying your agent or your treating doctor, hospital, or other health care provider orally or in writing of the revocation.

Your agent has the right to examine your medical records and to consent to their disclosure unless you limit this right in this document.

Unless you otherwise specify in this document, this document gives your agent the power after you die to (1) authorize an autopsy, (2) donate your body or parts thereof for transplant or therapeutic or educational or scientific purposes, and (3) direct the disposition of your remains.

If there is anything in this document that you do not understand, you should ask a lawyer to explain it to you.

(b) The printed form described in subdivision (a) shall also include the following notice:

"This power of attorney will not be valid for making health care decisions unless it is either (1) signed by two qualified adult witnesses who are present when you sign or acknowledge your signature or (2) acknowledged before a notary public in California."

(c) This section does not apply to the statutory form provided by Section 4771.

§ 4704. Durable power of attorney for health care not on printed form.

(a) A durable power of attorney prepared for execution by a person resident in this state that permits the attorney-in-fact to make health care decisions and that is not a printed form shall include one of the following:

(1) The substance of the statements provided in subdivision (a) of Section 4703 in capital letters.

(2) A certificate signed by the principal's lawyer stating: "I am a lawyer authorized to practice law in the state where this power of attorney was executed, and the principal was my client at the time this power of attorney was executed. I have advised my client concerning his or her rights in connection with this power of attorney and the applicable law and the consequences of signing or not signing this power of attorney, and my client, after being so advised, has executed this power of attorney."

(b) If a durable power of attorney includes the certificate provided for in paragraph (2) of subdivision (a) and permits the attorney-in-fact to make health care decisions for the principal, the applicable law of which the client is to be advised by the lawyer signing the certificate includes, but is not limited to, the matters listed in subdivision (a) of Section 4703.

SECTIONS 4720-4727

§ 4720. Health care decisions; priority of decisionmakers; standard of care.

(a) Unless the durable power of attorney provides otherwise, the attorney-in-fact designated in a durable power of attorney for health care who is known to the health care provider to be available and willing to make health care decisions has priority over any other person to act for the principal in all matters of health care decisions, but the attorney-in-fact does not have authority to make a particular health care decision if the principal is able to give informed consent with respect to that decision.

(b) Subject to any limitations in the durable power of attorney, the attorney-in-fact designated in a durable power of attorney for health care may make health care decisions for the principal, before or after the death of the principal, to the same extent as the principal could make health care decisions if the principal had the capacity to do so, including the following:

(1) Making a disposition under the Uniform Anatomical Gift Act (Chapter 3.5 (commencing with Section 7150) of Part 1 of Division 7 of the Health and Safety Code).

(2) Authorizing an autopsy under Section 7113 of the Health and Safety Code.

(3) Directing the disposition of remains under Section 7100 of the Health and Safety Code.

(c) In exercising the authority under the durable power of attorney for health care, the attorney-in-fact has a duty to act consistent with the desires of the principal as expressed in the durable power of attorney or otherwise made known to the attorney-in-fact at any time or, if the principal's desires are unknown, to act in the best interests of the principal.

(d) Nothing in this chapter affects any right the person designated as attorney-in-fact may have, apart from the durable power of attorney for health care, to make or participate in the making of health care decisions on behalf of the principal.

§ 4721. Medical information; attorney-in-fact's right to access.

Except to the extent the right is limited by the durable power of attorney for health care, an attorney-in-fact designated to make health care decisions under a durable power of attorney for health care has the same right as the principal to receive information regarding the proposed health care, to receive and review medical records, and to consent to the disclosure of medical records.

§ 4722. Consent; attorney-in-fact's authority.

A power of attorney may not authorize the attorney-in-fact to consent to any of the following on behalf of the principal:

(a) Commitment to or placement in a mental health treatment facility.

b) Convulsive treatment (as defined in Section 5325 of the Welfare and Institutions Code).

(c) Psychosurgery (as defined in Section 5325 of the Welfare and Institutions Code).

(d) Sterilization.

(e) Abortion.

§ 4723. Mercy killing; natural process of dying; attempted suicide.

Nothing in this chapter shall be construed to condone, authorize, or approve mercy killing, or to permit any affirmative or deliberate act or omission to end life other than the withholding or withdrawal of health care pursuant to a durable power of attorney for health care so as to permit the natural process of dying. In making health care decisions under a durable power of attorney for health care, an attempted suicide by the principal shall not be construed to indicate a desire of the principal that health care treatment be restricted or inhibited.

§ 4724. Principal's objections.

Nothing in this chapter authorizes an attorney-in-fact to consent to health care, or to consent to the withholding or withdrawal of health care necessary to keep the principal alive, if the principal objects to the health care or to the withholding or withdrawal of the health care. In such a case, the case is governed by the law that would apply if there were no durable power of attorney for health care.

§ 4725. Execution of durable power of attorney for health care as condition for medical treatment or insurance; prohibition.

No health care provider, health care service plan, insurer issuing disability insurance, self-insured employee welfare plan, or nonprofit hospital plan or similar insurance plan, may condition admission to a facility, or the providing of treatment, or insurance, on the requirement that a patient execute a durable power of attorney for health care.

§ 4726. Unlawful homicide; alteration or forgery of durable power of attorney; withholding or withdrawing necessary health care.

Any person who, except where justified or excused by law, alters or forges a durable power of attorney for health care of another, or willfully conceals or withholds personal knowledge of a revocation as provided under Section 4727, with the intent to cause a withholding or withdrawal of health care necessary to keep the principal alive contrary to the desires of the principal, and thereby, because of that act, directly causes health care necessary to keep the principal alive to be withheld or withdrawn and the death of the principal thereby to be hastened, is subject to prosecution for unlawful homicide as provided in Chapter 1 (commencing with Section 187) of Title 4 of Part 1 of the Penal Code.

§ 4727. Principal's power; revocation or attorney-in-fact's authority or durable power of attorney for health care; marriage dissolution or annulment; actual knowledge.

(a) At any time while the principal has the capacity to give a durable power of attorney for health care, the principal may do any of the following:

> (1) Revoke the appointment of the attorney-in-fact under the durable power of attorney for health care by notifying the attorney-in-fact orally or in writing.

> (2) Revoke the authority granted to the attorney-in-fact to make health care decisions by notifying the health care provider orally or in writing.

(b) If the principal notifies the health care provider orally or in writing that the authority granted to the attorney-in-fact to make health care decisions is revoked, the health care provider shall make the notification a part of the principal's medical records and shall make a reasonable effort to notify the attorney-in-fact of the revocation.

(c) It is presumed that the principal has the capacity to revoke a durable power of attorney for health care. This presumption is a presumption affecting the burden of proof.

(d) Unless it provides otherwise, a valid durable power of attorney for health care revokes any prior durable power of attorney for health care.

(e) Unless the durable power of attorney for health care expressly provides otherwise, if after executing a durable power of attorney for health care the principal's marriage is dissolved or annulled, the dissolution or annulment revokes any designation of the former spouse as an attorney-in-fact to make health care decisions for the principal. If any designation is revoked solely by this subdivision, it is revived by the principal's remarriage to the former spouse.

(f) If authority granted by a durable power of attorney for health care is revoked under this section, a person is not subject to criminal prosecution or civil liability for acting in good faith reliance upon the durable power of attorney for health care unless the person has actual knowledge of the revocation.

SECTIONS 4750-4753

§ 4750. Health care providers; immunities.

(a) Subject to any limitations stated in the durable power of attorney for health care and to subdivision (b) and to Sections 4722, 4723, 4724, 4725, and 4726, a health care provider is not subject to criminal prosecution, civil liability, or professional disciplinary action except to the same extent as would be the case if the principal, having had the capacity to give informed consent, had made the health care decision on his or her own behalf under like circumstances, if the health care provider relies on a health care decision and both of the following requirements are satisfied:

(1) The decision is made by an attorney-in-fact who the health care provider believes in good faith is authorized under this chapter to make the decision.

(2) The health care provider believes in good faith that the decision is not inconsistent with the desires of the principal as expressed in the durable power of attorney for health care or otherwise made known to the health care provider, and, if the decision is to withhold or withdraw health care necessary to keep the principal alive, the health care provider has made a good faith effort to determine the desires of the principal to the extent that the principal is able to convey those desires to the health care provider and the results of the effort are made a part of the principal's medical records.

(b) Nothing in this chapter authorizes a health care provider to do anything illegal.

(c) Notwithstanding the health care decision of the attorney-in-fact designated by a durable power of attorney for health care, the health care provider is not subject to criminal prosecution, civil liability, or professional disciplinary action for failing to withdraw health care necessary to keep the principal alive.

§ 4751. Declaration of witnesses; convincing evidence of principal's identity.

For the purposes of the declaration of witnesses required by Section 4701 or 4771, "convincing evidence" means the absence of any information, evidence, or other circumstances which would lead a reasonable person to believe that the person signing or acknowledging the durable power of attorney for health care as principal is not the individual he or she claims to be and any one of the following:

(a) Reasonable reliance on the presentation of any one of the following, if the document is current or has been issued within five years:

(1) An identification card or driver's license issued by the California Department of Motor Vehicles.

(2) A passport issued by the Department of State of the United States.

(b) Reasonable reliance on the presentation of any one of the following, if the document is current or has been issued within five years and contains a photograph and description of the person named on it, is signed by the person, bears a serial or other identifying number, and, in the event that the document is a passport, has been stamped by the United States Immigration and Naturalization Service:

(1) A passport issued by a foreign government.

(2) A driver's license issued by a state other than California or by a Canadian or Mexican public agency authorized to issue drivers' licenses.

(3) An identification card issued by a state other than California.

(4) An identification card issued by any branch of the armed forces of the United States.

(c) If the principal is a patient in a skilled nursing facility, a witness who is a patient advocate or ombudsman may, for the purposes of Section 4701 or 4771, rely upon the representations of the administrators or staff of the skilled nursing facility, or of family members, as convincing evidence of the identity of the principal if the patient advocate or ombudsman believes that the representations provide a reasonable basis for determining the identity of the principal.

§ 4752. Validity of durable power of attorney for health care; presumption.

In the absence of knowledge to the contrary, a physician and surgeon or other health care provider may presume that a durable power of attorney for health care or similar instrument, whether executed in another state or jurisdiction or in this state, is valid.

§ 4753. Requests to forego resuscitative measures; health care providers honoring requests; forms; contents; validity; application of section to current laws.

(a) A health care provider who honors a request to forego resuscitative measures, as defined in subdivision (b), shall not be subject to criminal prosecution, civil liability, discipline for unprofessional conduct, administrative sanction, or any other sanction, as a result of his or her reliance upon that request, if the health care provider: (1) believes in good faith that the action or decision is consistent with this section, and (2) has no knowledge that the action or decision would be inconsistent with a health care decision that the individual signing the request would have made on his or her own behalf under like circumstances.

(b) A "request to forego resuscitative measures" shall be a written document, signed by (1) the individual, or a legally recognized surrogate health care decisionmaker, and (2) a physician and surgeon, that directs a health care provider to forego resuscitative measures. For the purpose of this section, a "request to forego resuscitative measures" shall include a prehospital "do not resuscitate" form as developed by the Emergency Medical Services Authority or other substantially similar form. A request to forego resuscitative measures may also be evidenced by a medallion engraved with the words "do not resuscitate" or the letters "DNR", a patient identification number, and a 24-hour toll-free telephone number, issued by a person pursuant to an agreement with the Emergency Medical Services Authority.

(c) Request to forego resuscitative measures forms printed after January 1, 1995, shall contain the following:

"By signing this form, the surrogate acknowledges that this request to forego resuscitative measures is consistent with the known desires of, and with the best interest of, the individual who is the subject of the form."

(d) A substantially similar printed form shall be valid and enforceable if all of the following conditions are met:

(1) It is signed by the individual, or the individual's legally recognized surrogate health care decisionmaker, and a physician and surgeon.

(2) It directs health care providers to forego resuscitative measures.

(3) It contains all other information required by this section.

(e) In the absence of knowledge to the contrary, a health care provider may presume that a request to forego resuscitative measures is valid and unrevoked.

(f) This section shall apply whether the individual is within or outside a hospital or other health care facility.

(g) For purposes of this section "health care provider" shall include, but not be limited to, those persons described in Section 4615, and emergency response employees, including, but not limited to, firefighters, law enforcement officers, emergency medical technicians I and II, paramedics, or employees or volunteer members of legally organized and recognized volunteer organizations, who are trained in accordance with standards adopted as regulations by the Emergency Medical Services Authority pursuant to Sections 1797.170, 1797.171, 1797.172, 1797.182, and 1797.183 of the Health and Safety Code to respond to medical emergencies in the course of performing their volunteer or employee duties with the organization.

(h) This section does not repeal or narrow current laws relating to health care decisionmaking, including the provisions governing the use of the Durable Power of Attorney for Health Care contained in this chapter, and the provisions relating to the use of declarations concerning life sustaining treatments pursuant to the Natural Death Act (Chapter 3.9 (commencing with Section 7185) of Part 1 of Division 7 of the Health and Safety Code).

SECTIONS 4770-4779

§ 4770. Short title.

This chapter shall be known and may be cited as the Keene Health Care Agent Act.

§ 4771. Form.

The use of the following form in the creation of a durable power of attorney for health care under Chapter 1 (commencing with Section 4600) is lawful, and when used, the power of attorney shall be construed in accordance with this chapter and is subject to Chapter 1 (commencing with Section 4600), provided, however, that the use of a form previously authorized by this statute (at the time it was so authorized) remains valid.

[See Form C in appendix B

and Form 3 in appendix C]

§ 4772. Warning statement; certificate of principal's lawyer.

(a) Notwithstanding Section 4703, except as provided in subdivision (b), a statutory form durable power of attorney for health care, to be valid, shall contain, in not less than 10-point boldface type or a reasonable equivalent thereof, the warning statement that is set forth in capital letters at the beginning of Section 4771.

(b) Subdivision (a) does not apply if the statutory form durable power of attorney for health care contains a certificate signed by the principal's lawyer stating the following: "I am a lawyer authorized to practice law in the state where this power of attorney was executed, and the principal was my client at the time when this power of attorney was executed. I have advised my client concerning his or her rights in connection with this power of attorney and the applicable law and the consequences of signing or not signing this power of attorney, and my client, after being so advised, has executed this power of attorney."

§ 4773. Validity of form.

(a) Notwithstanding subdivision (c) of Section 4121, a statutory form durable power of attorney for health care is valid, and the designated attorney-in-fact may make health care decisions pursuant to its authority, only if it (1) contains the date of its execution, (2) is signed by the principal, and (3) is signed by two qualified witnesses, each of whom executes, under penalty of perjury, the declaration set forth in the first paragraph of the "Statement of Witnesses" in the form set forth in Section 4771, and one of whom also executes the declaration under penalty of perjury set forth in the second paragraph of the "Statement of Witnesses" in the form set forth in Section 4771.

(b) Nothing in this section excuses compliance with the special requirements imposed by subdivision (e) of Section 4701 and subdivision (d) of Section 4702.

§ 4774. Creation of statutory form; sale or distribution of printed forms; execution of additional pages.

(a) Subject to subdivisions (b), (c), and (d), a power of attorney is a "statutory form durable power of attorney for health care," as this phrase is used in this chapter, if it meets both of the following requirements:

(1) It meets the requirements of Sections 4772 and 4773.

(2) It includes the exact wording of the text of paragraphs 1, 2, 3, and 4 of the form set forth in Section 4771.

(b) A statutory form durable power of attorney for health care may include one or more or all of paragraphs 5 to 11, inclusive, of the form set forth in Section 4771.

(c) A printed statutory form durable power of attorney for health care sold or otherwise distributed in this state for use by a person who does not have the advice of legal counsel shall contain the exact wording of the form set forth in Section 4771, including the warning and instructions, and nothing else. Nothing in this subdivision prohibits selling or otherwise distributing with the printed form (1) material that explains the form and its use if the material is separate from the printed form itself and is not a part of the form executed by the principal or (2) one or more additional pages that are separate from the printed form itself that a person may attach to the printed form as provided in subdivision (d) if the person so chooses.

(d) If one or more additional pages are attached to a statutory form durable power of attorney for health care as a statement, or additional statement, to be a part of subparagraph (a) or (b), or both, of paragraph 4 ("Statement of Desires, Special Provisions, and Limitations") of the form set forth in Section 4771, each of the additional pages shall be dated and signed by the principal at the same time the principal dates and signs the statutory form durable power of attorney for health care.

§ 4775. Forms executed under prior law; validity; warning language; sale or distribution of printed forms.

(a) A statutory form durable power of attorney for health care executed on or after January 1, 1992, using a form that complies with former Section 2500 of the Civil Code is as valid as if it had been executed using a form that complies with Section 4771 of this code.

(b) Notwithstanding former Section 2501 of the Civil Code or Section 4772 of this code, a statutory form durable power of attorney for health care executed on or after January 1, 1992, is not invalid if it contains the warning using the language set forth in former Section 2500 of the Civil Code instead of the warning using the language set forth in Section 4771 of this code.

(c) For the purposes of subdivision (c) of former Section 2503 of the Civil Code and subdivision (c) of Section 4774 of this code, on and after January 1, 1992, a printed statutory form durable power of attorney for health care may be sold or otherwise distributed if it contains the exact wording of the form set forth in former Section 2500 of the Civil Code or the exact wording of the form set forth in Section 4771 of this code, including the warning and instructions, and nothing else; but any printed statutory form durable power of attorney for health care printed on or after January 1, 1992, that is sold or otherwise distributed in this state for use by a person who does not have the advice of legal counsel shall contain the exact wording of the form set forth in former Section 2500 of the Civil Code or the exact wording of the form set forth in Section 4771

of this code, including the warning and instructions, and nothing else.

§ 4776. Form language regarding health care decisions; scope of authority in selection and discharge of health care professionals.

In a statutory form durable power of attorney for health care, the language conferring general authority with respect to "health care decisions" authorizes the attorney-in-fact to select and discharge physicians, dentists, nurses, therapists, and other health care professionals as the attorney-in-fact determines necessary to carry out the health care decisions the attorney-in-fact is authorized by the power of attorney to make.

§ 4777. Execution of document under authority granted in statutory form.

If a document described in paragraph 5 or 6 of the form set forth in Section 4771 is executed on behalf of the principal by the attorney-in-fact in the exercise of authority granted to the attorney-in-fact by paragraph 5 or 6 of the form set forth in Section 4771, the document has the same effect as if the principal had executed the document at the same time and under the same circumstances and had the capacity to execute the document at that time.

§ 4778. Termination of attorney-in-fact's authority; alternate attorney-in-fact.

If the authority of the attorney-in-fact under the statutory form durable power of attorney for health care is terminated by the court under Part 5 (commencing with Section 4900), an alternate attorney-in-fact designated in the statutory form durable power of attorney for health care is not authorized to act as the attorney-in-fact unless the court so orders. In the order terminating the authority of the attorney-in-fact to make health care decisions for the principal, the court shall authorize the alternate attorney-in-fact, if any, designated in the statutory form durable power of attorney for health care to act as the attorney-in-fact to make health care decisions for the principal under the durable power of attorney for health care unless the court finds that authorizing that alternate attorney-in-fact to make health care decisions for the principal would not be in the best interests of the principal.

§ 4779. Alternate forms; application of chapter.

Nothing in this chapter affects or limits the use of any other form for a durable power of attorney for health care. Any form complying with the requirements of Chapter 1 (commencing with Section 4600) may be used in lieu of the form provided by Section 4771, and none of the provisions of this chapter apply if the other form is used.

SECTIONS 4800-4806

§ 4800. Registry system.

The Secretary of State shall establish a registry system by which any person who has executed a durable power of attorney for health care may register in a central information center information regarding the durable power of attorney for health care, making that information available upon request to any health care provider, the public guardian, or other person authorized by the registrant. Information that may be received and released is limited to the registrant's name, social security or driver's license or other individual identifying number established by law, if any, address, date and place of birth, the intended place of deposit or safekeeping of the durable power of attorney for health care, and the name and telephone number of the attorney in fact and any alternative attorney in fact. The Secretary of State, at the request of the registrant, may transmit the information he or she receives regarding the durable power of attorney for health care to the registry system of another jurisdiction as identified by the registrant. The Secretary of State may charge a fee to each registrant in an amount such that, when all fees charged to registrants are aggregated, the aggregated fees do not exceed the actual cost of establishing and maintaining the registry.

§ 4801. Authorized persons requesting information; verification; procedures.

The Secretary of State shall establish procedures to verify the identities of health care providers, the public guardian, and other authorized persons requesting information pursuant to Section 4800. No fee shall be charged to any health care provider, the public guardian, or other authorized person requesting information pursuant to Section 4800.

§ 4802. Advice to registrants; procedures.

The Secretary of State shall establish procedures to advise each registrant of the following:

(a) A health care provider may not honor a durable power of attorney for health care until it receives a copy from the registrant.

(b) Each registrant must notify the registry upon revocation of the durable power of attorney for health care.

(c) Each registrant must reregister upon execution of a subsequent durable power of attorney for health care.

§ 4804. Failure to register.

Failure to register with the Secretary of State shall not invalidate any durable power of attorney for health care.

§ 4805. Effect of registration.

Registration with the Secretary of State shall not affect the ability of the registrant to revoke that durable power of attorney cr a later executed power, nor shall registration raise any presumption of validity or superiority among any competing powers or revocations.

§ 4806. Construction of chapter; duties of health care providers.

Nothing in this chapter shall be construed to require a health care provider to request from the registry information about whether a patient has executed a durable power of attorney for health care. Nothing in this chapter shall be construed to affect the duty of a health care provider to provide information to a patient regarding advance health care directives pursuant to any provision of federal law.

SECTIONS 4900-4905

§ 4900. Judicial intervention.

A power of attorney is exercisable free of judicial intervention, subject to this part.

§ 4901. Remedies.

The remedies provided in this part are cumulative and not exclusive of any other remedies provided by law.

§ 4902. Limitations.

Except as provided in Section 4903, this part is not subject to limitation in the power of attorney.

§ 4903. Authority to petition court; expressed limitation in power of attorney.

(a) Subject to subdivision (b), a power of attorney may expressly eliminate the authority of a person listed in Section 4940 to petition the court for any one or more of the purposes enumerated in Section 4941 or 4942 if both of the following requirements are satisfied:

(1) The power of attorney is executed by the principal at a time when the principal has the advice of a lawyer authorized to practice law in the state where the power of attorney is executed.

(2) The principal's lawyer signs a certificate stating in substance:

"I am a lawyer authorized to practice law in the state where this power of attorney was executed, and the principal was my client at the time this power of attorney was executed. I have advised my client concerning his or her rights in connection with this power of attorney and the applicable law and the consequences of signing or not signing this power of attorney, and my client, after being so advised, has executed this power of attorney."

(b) A power of attorney may not limit the authority of the following persons to petition under this part:

(1) The attorney-in-fact, the principal, the conservator of the estate of the principal, or the public guardian, with respect to a petition for a purpose specified in Section 4941.

(2) The conservator of the person of the principal, with respect to a petition relating to a durable

power of attorney for health care for a purpose specified in subdivision (a), (c), or (d) of Section 4942.

(3) The attorney-in-fact, with respect to a petition relating to a durable power of attorney for health care for a purpose specified in subdivision (a) or (b) of Section 4942.

§ 4904. Right to jury trial.

There is no right to a jury trial in proceedings under this division.

§ 4905. Application of other laws.

Except as otherwise provided in this division, the general provisions in Division 3 (commencing with Section 1000) apply to proceedings under this division.

SECTIONS 4920-4923

§ 4920. Jurisdiction; power of court.

(a) The superior court has jurisdiction in proceedings under this division.

(b) The court in proceedings under this division is a court of general jurisdiction and the court, or a judge of the court, has the same power and authority with respect to the proceedings as otherwise provided by law for a superior court, or a judge of the superior court, including, but not limited to, the matters authorized by Section 128 of the Code of Civil Procedure.

§ 4921. Exercise of jurisdiction.

The court may exercise jurisdiction in proceedings under this division on any basis permitted by Section 410.10 of the Code of Civil Procedure.

§ 4922. Personal jurisdiction over acting attorney-in-fact.

Without limiting Section 4921, a person who acts as an attorney-in-fact under a power of attorney governed by this division is subject to personal jurisdiction in this state with respect to matters relating to acts and transactions of the attorney-in-fact performed in this state or affecting property or a principal in this state.

§ 4923. Venue; order of priority.

The proper county for commencement of a proceeding under this division shall be determined in the following order of priority:

(a) The county in which the principal resides.

(b) The county in which the attorney-in-fact resides.

(c) A county in which property subject to the power of attorney is located.

(d) Any other county that is in the principal's best interest.

SECTIONS 4940-4947

§ 4940. Petitioners.

Subject to Section 4903, a petition may be filed under this part by any of the following persons:

(a) The attorney-in-fact.

(b) The principal.

(c) The spouse of the principal.

(d) A relative of the principal.

(e) The conservator of the person or estate of the principal.

(f) The court investigator, described in Section 1454, of the county where the power of attorney was executed or where the principal resides.

(g) The public guardian of the county where the power of attorney was executed or where the principal resides.

(h) A treating health care provider, with respect to a durable power of attorney for health care.

(i) The personal representative or trustee of the principal's estate.

(j) The principal's successor in interest.

(k) A person who is requested in writing by an attorney-in-fact to take action.

(l) Any other interested person or friend of the principal.

§ 4941. Petition; purposes.

With respect to a power of attorney other than a durable power of attorney for health care, a petition may be filed under this part for any one or more of the following purposes:

(a) Determining whether the power of attorney is in effect or has terminated.

(b) Passing on the acts or proposed acts of the attorney-in-fact, including approval of authority to disobey the principal's instructions pursuant to subdivision (b) of Section 4234.

(c) Compelling the attorney-in-fact to submit the attorney-in-fact's accounts or report the attorney-in-fact's acts as attorney-in-fact to the principal, the spouse of the principal, the conservator of the person or the estate of the principal, or to any other person required by the court in its discretion, if the attorney-in-fact has failed to submit an accounting or report within 60 days after written request from the person filing the petition.

(d) Declaring that the authority of the attorney-in-fact is revoked on a determination by the court of all of the following:

(1) The attorney-in-fact has violated or is unfit to perform the fiduciary duties under the power of attorney.

(2) At the time of the determination by the court, the principal lacks the capacity to give or to revoke a power of attorney.

(3) The revocation of the attorney-in-fact's authority is in the best interest of the principal or the principal's estate.

(e) Approving the resignation of the attorney-in-fact:

(1) If the attorney-in-fact is subject to a duty to act under Section 4230, the court may approve the resignation, subject to any orders the court determines are necessary to protect the principal's interests.

(2) If the attorney-in-fact is not subject to a duty to act under Section 4230, the court shall approve the resignation, subject to the court's discretion to require the attorney-in-fact to give notice to other interested persons.

(f) Compelling a third person to honor the authority of an attorney-in-fact.

§ 4942. Petition regarding durable power of attorney for health care; purpose.

With respect to a durable power of attorney for health care, a petition may be filed under this part for any one or more of the following purposes:

(a) Determining whether the durable power of attorney for health care is in effect or has terminated.

(b) Determining whether the acts or pro0posed acts of the attorney-in-fact are consistent with the desires of the principal as expressed in the durable power of attorney for health care or otherwise made known to the court or, where the desires of the principal are unknown or unclear, whether the acts or proposed acts of the attorney-in-fact are in the best interests of the principal.

(c) Compelling the attorney-in-fact to report the attorney-in-fact' s acts as attorney-in-fact to the principal, the spouse of the principal, the conservator of the person of the principal, or to any other person required by the court in its discretion, if the attorney-in-fact has failed to submit the report within 10 days after written request from the person filing the petition.

(d) Declaring that the durable power of attorney for health care is terminated upon a determination by the court that the attorney-in-fact has made a health care decision for the principal that authorized anything illegal or upon a determination by the court of both of the following:

(1) The attorney-in-fact has violated, has failed to perform, or is unfit to perform, the duty under the durable power of attorney for health care to act consistent with the desires of the principal or, where the desires of the principal are unknown or unclear, is acting (by action or inaction) in a manner that is clearly contrary to the best interests of the principal.

(2) At the time of the determination by the court, the principal lacks the capacity to execute or to revoke a durable power of attorney for health care.

(e) Approving the resignation of the attorney-in-fact:

(1) If the attorney-in-fact is subject to a duty to act under Section 4230, the court may approve the resignation, subject to any orders the court determines are necessary to protect the principal's interests.

(2) If the attorney-in-fact is not subject to a duty to act under Section 4230, the court shall approve the resignation, subject to the court's discretion to require the attorney-in-fact to give notice to other interested persons.

§ 4943. Contents of petition.

A proceeding under this part is commenced by filing a petition stating facts showing that the petition is authorized under this part, the grounds of the petition, and, if known to the petitioner, the terms of the power of attorney.

§ 4944. Dismissal of petition; stay or dismissal of proceeding.

The court may dismiss a petition if it appears that the proceeding is not reasonably necessary for the protection of the interests of the principal or the principal's estate and shall stay or dismiss the proceeding in whole or in part when required by Section 410.30 of the Code of Civil Procedure.

§ 4945. Hearing; notice.

(a) Subject to subdivision (b), at least 15 days before the time set for hearing, the petitioner shall serve notice of the time and place of the hearing, together with a copy of the petition, on the following:

(1) The attorney-in-fact if not the petitioner.

(2) The principal if not the petitioner.

(b) In the case of a petition to compel a third person to honor the authority of an attorney-in-fact, notice of the time and place of the hearing, together with a copy of the petition, shall be served on the third person in the manner provided in Chapter 4 (commencing with Section 413.10) of Title 5 of Part 2 of the Code of Civil Procedure.

§ 4946. Temporary order prescribing health care of principal.

With respect to a durable power of attorney for health care, the court in its discretion, upon a showing of good cause, may issue a temporary order prescribing the health care of the principal until the disposition of the petition filed under Section 4942. If a durable power of attorney for health care is in effect and a conservator (including a temporary conservator) of the person is appointed for the principal, the court that appoints the conservator in its discretion, upon a showing of good cause, may issue a temporary order prescribing the health care of the principal, that order to continue in effect for such time as is ordered by the court but in no case longer than the time necessary to permit the filing and determination of a petition filed under Section 4942.

§ 4947. Attorney's fees.

In a proceeding under this part commenced by the filing of a petition by a person other than the attorney-in-fact, the court may in its discretion award reasonable attorney's fees to one of the following:

(a) The attorney-in-fact, if the court determines that the proceeding was commenced without any reasonable cause.

(b) The person commencing the proceeding, if the court determines that the attorney-in-fact has clearly violated the fiduciary duties under the power of attorney or has failed without any reasonable cause or justification to submit accounts or report acts to the principal or conservator of the estate or of the person, as the case may be, after written request from the principal or conservator.

SECTION 5204

§ 5204. Special power of attorney; institution liability upon reliance on validity; records fro accounting; attorney liability; application of other laws.

(a) In addition to a power of attorney otherwise authorized by law, a special power of attorney is authorized under this section to apply to one or more accounts at a financial institution or to one or more contracts with a financial institution concerning safe deposit services. For the purposes of this section, "account" includes checking accounts, savings accounts, certificates of deposit, savings certificates, and any other depository relationship with the financial institution.

(b) The special power of attorney under this section shall:

(1) Be in writing.

(2) Be signed by the person or persons giving the power of attorney.

(3) Explicitly identify the attorney-in-fact or attorneys-in-fact, the financial institution, and the accounts or contracts subject to the power.

(c) The special power of attorney shall contain language in substantially the following form:

"WARNING TO PERSON EXECUTING THIS DOCUMENT: This is an important legal document. It creates a power of attorney that provides the person you designate as your attorney-in-fact with the broad powers it sets forth. You have the right to terminate this power of attorney. If there is anything about this form that you do not understand, you should ask a lawyer to explain it to you."

(d) In addition to the language required by subdivision (c), special powers of attorney that are or may be durable shall also contain substantially the following language:

"These powers of attorney shall continue even if you later become disabled or incapacitated."

(e) The power of attorney granted under this section shall endure as between the grantor and grantee of the power until the earliest of the following occurs:

(1) Revocation by the grantor of the power.

(2) Termination of the account.

(3) Death of the grantor of the power.

(4) In the case of a nondurable power of attorney, appointment of a guardian or conservator of the estate of the grantor of the power.

(f) A financial institution may rely in good faith upon the validity of the power of attorney granted under this section and is not liable to the principal or any other person for doing so if (1) the power of attorney is on file with the financial institution and the transaction is made by the attorney-in-fact named in the power of attorney, (2) the power of attorney appears on its face to be valid, and (3) the financial institution has convincing evidence of the identity of the person signing the power of attorney as principal. (g) For the purposes of subdivision (f), "convincing evidence" requires both of the following:

(1) Reasonable reliance on a document that satisfies the requirement of Section 4751.

(2) The absence of any information, evidence, or other circumstances that would lead a reasonable person to believe that the person signing the power of attorney as principal is not the individual he or she claims to be.

(h) The protection provided by subdivision (f) does not extend to payments made after written notice is received by the financial institution as to any of the events of termination of the power under subdivision (e) if the financial institution has had a reasonable time to act on the notice. No other notice or any other information shown to have been available to the financial institution shall affect its right to the protection provided by this subdivision.

(i) The attorney-in-fact acting under the power of attorney granted under this section shall maintain books or records to permit an accounting of the acts of the attorney-in-fact if an accounting is requested by a legal representative of the grantor of the power.

(j) The attorney-in-fact acting under a power of attorney granted under this section is liable for any disbursement other than a disbursement to or for the benefit of the grantor of the power, unless the grantor has authorized the disbursement in writing.

(k) Nothing in this section limits the use or effect of any other form of power of attorney for transactions with a financial institution. Nothing in this section creates an implication that a financial institution is liable for acting in reliance upon a power of attorney under circumstances where the requirements of subdivision (f) are not satisfied. Nothing in this section affects any immunity that may otherwise exist apart from this section.

(l) Nothing in this section prevents the attorney-in-fact from also being designated as a P.O.D. payee.

(m) Except as otherwise provided in this section, the Power of Attorney Law, Division 4.5 (commencing with Section 4000) shall not apply to a special power of attorney under this section. Section 4130 and Part 5 (commencing with Section 4900) of Division 4.5 shall apply to a special power of attorney under this section.

HEALTH AND SAFETY CODE

SECTIONS 7185-7194.5

§ 7185. Short title.

This act shall be known and may be cited as the Natural Death Act.

§ 7185.5. Legislative findings and declaration.

(a) The Legislature finds that an adult person has the fundamental right to control the decisions relating to the rendering of his or her own medical care, including the decision to have life-sustaining treatment withheld or withdrawn in instances of a terminal condition or permanent unconscious condition.

(b) The Legislature further finds that modern medical technology has made possible the artificial prolongation of human life beyond natural limits.

(c) The Legislature further finds that, in the interest of protecting individual autonomy, such prolongation of the process of dying for a person with a terminal condition or permanent unconscious condition for whom continued medical treatment does not improve the prognosis for recovery may violate patient dignity and cause unnecessary pain and suffering, while providing nothing medically necessary or beneficial to the person.

(d) In recognition of the dignity and privacy that a person has a right to expect, the Legislature hereby declares that the laws of the State of California shall recognize the right of an adult person to make a written declaration instructing his or her physician to withhold or withdraw life-sustaining treatment in the event of a terminal condition or permanent unconscious condition, in the event that the person is unable to make those decisions for himself or herself.

(e) The Legislature further declares that, in the absence of controversy, a court normally is not the proper forum in which to make decisions regarding life-sustaining treatment.

(f) To avoid treatment that is not desired by a person in a terminal condition or permanent unconscious condition, the Legislature declares that this chapter is in the interest of the public health and welfare.

§ 7186. Definitions.

As used in this chapter, unless the context otherwise requires:

(a) "Attending physician" means the physician who has primary responsibility for the treatment and care of the patient.

(b) "Declaration" means a writing executed in accordance with the requirements of subdivision (a) of Section 7186.5.

(c) "Health care provider" means a person who is licensed, certified, or otherwise authorized by the law of this state to administer health care in the ordinary course of business or practice of a profession.

(d) "Life-sustaining treatment" means any medical procedure or intervention that, when administered to a qualified patient, will serve only to prolong the process of dying or an irreversible coma or persistent vegetative state.

(e) "Permanent unconscious condition" means an incurable and irreversible condition that, within reasonable medical judgment, renders the patient in an irreversible coma or persistent vegetative state.

(f) "Person" means an individual, corporation, business trust, estate, trust, partnership, limited liability company, association, joint venture, government, governmental subdivision or agency, or any other legal or commercial entity.

(g) "Physician" means a physician and surgeon licensed by the Medical Board of California or the Osteopathic Medical Board of California.

(h) "Qualified patient" means a patient 18 or more years of age who has executed a declaration and who has been diagnosed and certified in writing by the attending physician and a second physician who has personally examined the patient to be in a terminal condition or permanent unconscious condition.

(i) "State" means a state of the United States, the District of Columbia, the Commonwealth of Puerto Rico, or a territory or insular possession subject to the jurisdiction of the United States.

(j) "Terminal condition" means an incurable and irreversible condition that, without the administration of life-sustaining treatment, will, within reasonable medical judgment, result in death within a relatively short time.

§ 7186.5. Declarations concerning life-sustaining treatment; execution requirements.

(a) An individual of sound mind and 18 or more years of age may execute at any time a declaration governing the withholding or withdrawal of life-sustaining treatment. The declaration shall be signed by the declarant, or another at the declarant's direction and in the declarant's presence, and witnessed by two individuals at least one of whom may not be a person who is entitled to any portion of the estate of the qualified patient upon his or her death under any will or codicil thereto of the qualified patient existing at the time of execution of the declaration or by operation of law. In addition, a health care provider, an employee of a health care provider, the operator of a community care facility, an employee of an operator of a community care facility, the operator of a residential care facility for the elderly, or an employee of an operator of a residential care facility for the elderly may not be a witness.

(b) A declaration shall substantially contain the following provisions:

*[See Form C in appendix B
and Form 3 in appendix C]*

(c) A physician or other health care provider who is furnished a copy of the declaration shall make it a part of the declarant's medical record and, if unwilling to comply with the declaration, promptly so advise the declarant.

§ 7187. Patients in skilled nursing facilities or long-term health facilities; effect of declaration.

A declaration shall have no force or effect if the declarant is a patient in a skilled nursing facility as defined in subdivision (c) of Section 1250, or a long-term health care facility as defined in subdivision (a) of Section 1418, at the time the declaration is executed unless one of the two witnesses to the declaration is a patient advocate or ombudsman as may be designated by the State Department of Aging for this purpose pursuant to any other applicable provision of law.

§ 7187.5. Operative effect of declaration.

A declaration becomes operative when (a) it is communicated to the attending physician and (b) the declarant is diagnosed and certified in writing by the attending physician and a second physician who has personally examined the declarant to be in a terminal condition or permanent unconscious condition and no longer able to make decisions regarding administration of life-sustaining treatment. When the declaration becomes operative, the attending physician and other health care providers shall act in accordance with its provisions or comply with the transfer requirements of Section 7190.

§ 7188. Revocation of declaration.

(a) A declarant may revoke a declaration at any time and in any manner, without regard to the declarant's mental or physical condition. A revocation is effective upon its communication to the attending physician or other health care provider by the declarant or a witness to the revocation.

(b) The attending physician or other health care provider shall make the revocation a part of the declarant's medical record.

§ 7189. Terminal or permanent unconscious condition; records.

Upon determining that the declarant is in a terminal condition or permanent unconscious condition, the attending physician who knows of a declaration shall record the determination and the terms of the declaration in the declarant's medical record and file a copy of the declaration in the record.

§ 7189.5. Self-determination by patient; pregnant patients.

(a) A qualified patient may make decisions regarding life-sustaining treatment as long as the patient is able to do so.

(b) This chapter does not affect the responsibility of the attending physician or other health care provider to provide treatment for a patient's comfort care or alleviation of pain.

(c) The declaration of a qualified patient known to the attending physician to be pregnant shall not be given effect as long as the patient is pregnant.

§ 7190. Physician or health care provider unwilling to comply with chapter; transfer of patient.

An attending physician or other health care provider who is unwilling to comply with this chapter shall take all reasonable steps as promptly as practicable to transfer care of the declarant to another physician or health care provider who is willing to do so.

§ 7190.5. Civil or criminal liability; unprofessional conduct.

(a) A physician or other health care provider is not subject to civil or criminal liability, or discipline for unprofessional conduct, for giving effect to a declaration in the absence of knowledge of the revocation of a declaration.

(b) A physician or other health care provider, whose action under this chapter is in accord with reasonable medical standards, is not subject to criminal prosecution, civil liability, discipline for unprofessional conduct, administrative sanction, or any other sanction if the physician or health care provider believes in good faith that the action is consistent with this chapter and the desires of the declarant expressed in the declaration.

§ 7191. Willful failure to act; fraudulent conduct; penalties.

(a) A physician or other health care provider who willfully fails to transfer the care of a patient in accordance with Section 7190 is guilty of a misdemeanor.

(b) A physician who willfully fails to record a determination of terminal condition or permanent unconscious condition or the terms of a declaration in accordance with Section 7189 is guilty of a misdemeanor.

(c) An individual who willfully conceals, cancels, defaces, or obliterates the declaration of another individual without the declarant's consent or who falsifies or forges a revocation of the declaration of another individual is guilty of a misdemeanor.

(d) An individual who falsifies or forges the declaration of another individual, or willfully conceals or withholds personal knowledge of a revocation under Section 7188, with the intent to cause a withholding or withdrawal of life-sustaining treatment contrary to the wishes of the declarant, and thereby, because of that act, directly causes life-sustaining treatment to be withheld or withdrawn and death to thereby be hastened, shall be subject to prosecution for unlawful homicide as provided in Chapter 1 (commencing with Section 187) of Title 8 of Part 1 of the Penal Code.

(e) A person who requires or prohibits the execution of a declaration as a condition for being insured for, or receiving, health care services is guilty of a misdemeanor.

(f) A person who coerces or fraudulently induces an individual to execute a declaration is guilty of a misdemeanor.

(g) The sanctions provided in this section do not displace any sanction applicable under other law.

§ 7191.5. Construction of chapter; characterization of death resulting from decisions made in accordance with chapter; effect of declaration on life insurance or annuities; deliberate acts or omissions to end life.

(a) Death resulting from the withholding or withdrawal of a life-sustaining treatment in accordance with this chapter does not constitute, for any purpose, a suicide or homicide.

(b) The making of a declaration pursuant to Section 7186.5 does not affect in any manner the sale, procurement, or issuance of any policy of life insurance or annuity, nor does it affect, impair, or modify the terms of an existing policy of life insurance or annuity. A policy of life insurance or annuity is not legally impaired or invalidated by the withholding or withdrawal of life-sustaining treatment from an insured, notwithstanding any term to the contrary.

(c) A person may not prohibit or require the execution of a declaration as a condition for being insured for, or receiving, health care services.

(d) This chapter creates no presumption concerning the intention of an individual who has revoked or has not executed a declaration with respect to the use, withholding, or withdrawal of life-sustaining treatment in the event of a terminal condition or permanent unconscious condition.

(e) This chapter does not affect the right of a patient to make decisions regarding use of life-sustaining treatment, so long as the patient is able to do so, or impair or supersede a right or responsibility that a person has to effect the withholding or withdrawal of medical care.

(f) This chapter does not require any physician or other health care provider to take any action contrary to reasonable medical standards.

(g) This chapter does not condone, authorize, or approve mercy killing or assisted suicide or permit any affirmative or deliberate act or omission to end life other than to permit the natural process of dying.

(h) The rights granted by this chapter are in addition to, and not in derogation of, rights under any other statutory or case law.

§ 7192. Declaration presumed in compliance and valid.

In the absence of knowledge to the contrary, a physician or other health care provider may presume that a declaration complies with this chapter and is valid.

§ 7192.5. Instruments executed in other states.

An instrument governing the withholding or withdrawal of life-sustaining treatment executed in another state in compliance with the law of that state or of this state is valid for purposes of this chapter.

§ 7193. Durable Power of Attorney for Health Care; relationship to declaration.

A Durable Power of Attorney for Health Care shall prevail over a declaration executed pursuant to this chapter unless expressly provided otherwise in the Durable Power of Attorney for Health Care.

§ 7193.5. Instruments to be given effect pursuant to chapter.

The following instruments shall be given effect pursuant to the provisions of this chapter:

(a) An instrument executed before January 1, 1992, that substantially complies with subdivision (a) of Section 7186.5.

(b) An instrument governing the withholding or withdrawal of life-sustaining treatment executed in another state that does not comply with the law of that state but substantially complies with the law of this state.

§ 7194. If any provision of this chapter or its application to any person or circumstance is held invalid, the invalidity shall not affect other provisions or applications of this chapter which can be given effect without the invalid provision or application, and to this end the provisions of this chapter are severable.

§ 7194.5. To the extent that a provision of this chapter conforms to the Uniform Rights of the Terminally Ill Act, that provision shall be applied and construed to effectuate its general purpose to make uniform the law with respect to the subject of this chapter among states enacting it.

FAMILY CODE

SECTIONS 6550-6552

§ 6550. Authorization affidavits; scope of authority; reliance on affidavit.

(a) A caregiver's authorization affidavit that meets the requirements of this part authorizes a caregiver 18 years of age or older who completes items 1-4 of the affidavit provided in Section 6552 and signs the affidavit to enroll a minor in school and consent to school-related medical care on behalf of the minor. A caregiver who is a relative and who completes items 1-8 of the affidavit provided in Section 6552 and signs the affidavit shall have the same rights to authorize medical care and dental care for the minor that are given to guardians under Section 2353 of the Probate Code. The medical care authorized by this caregiver who is a relative may include mental health treatment subject to the limitations of Section

2356 of the Probate Code.

(b) The affidavit shall not be valid for more than one year after the date on which it is executed.

(c) The decision of a caregiver to consent to or to refuse medical or dental care for a minor shall be superseded by any contravening decision of the parent or other person having legal custody of the minor, provided the decision of the parent or other person having legal custody of the minor does not jeopardize the life, health, or safety of the minor.

(d) No person who acts in good faith reliance on a caregiver's authorization affidavit to provide medical or dental care, without actual knowledge of facts contrary to those stated on the affidavit, is subject to criminal liability or to civil liability to any person, or is subject to professional disciplinary action, for such reliance if the applicable portions of the affidavit are completed.

This subdivision shall apply even if medical or dental care is provided to a minor in contravention of the wishes of the parent or other person having legal custody of the minor as long as the person providing the medical or dental care has no actual knowledge of the wishes of the parent or other person having legal custody of the minor.

(e) A person who relies on the affidavit has no obligation to make any further inquiry or investigation.

(f) Nothing in this section shall relieve any individual from liability for violations of other provisions of law.

(g) If the minor stops living with the caregiver, the caregiver shall notify any school, health care provider, or health care service plan that has been given the affidavit.

(h) A caregiver's authorization affidavit shall be invalid unless it substantially contains, in not less than 10-point boldface type or a reasonable equivalent thereof, the warning statement beginning with the word "warning" specified in Section 6552. The warning statement shall be enclosed in a box with 3-point rule lines.

(i) For purposes of this part:

(1) "Person" includes an individual, corporation, partnership, association, the state, or any city, county, city and county, or other public entity or governmental subdivision or agency, or any other legal entity.

(2) "Relative" means a spouse, parent, stepparent, brother, sister, stepbrother, stepsister, half-brother, half-sister, uncle, aunt, niece, nephew, first cousin, or any person denoted by the prefix "grand" or "great," or the spouse of any of the persons specified in this definition, even after the marriage has been terminated by death or dissolution.

(3) "School-related medical care" means medical care that is required by state or local governmental authority as a condition for school enrollment, including immunizations, physical examinations, and medical examinations conducted in schools for pupils.

§ 6552. Form of authorization affidavit.

The caregiver's authorization affidavit shall be insubstantially the following form:

Caregiver's Authorization Affidavit

Use of this affidavit is authorized by Part 1.5 (commencing with Section 6550) of Division 11 of the California Family Code.

Instructions: Completion of items 1-4 and the signing of the affidavit is sufficient to authorize enrollment of a minor in school and authorize school-related medical care. Completion of items 5-8 is additionally required to authorize any other medical care. Print clearly.

The minor named below lives in my home and I am 18 years of age or older.

1. Name of minor: _________________________.

2. Minor's birth date: ___________________.

3. My name (adult giving authorization):

_________________________________.

4. My home address:

____

_________________________________.

5. ( ) I am a grandparent, aunt, uncle, or other qualified relative of the minor (see back of this form for a definition of "qualified relative").

6. Check one or both (for example, if one parent was advised and the other cannot be located):

( ) I have advised the parent(s) or other person(s) having legal custody of the minor of my intent to authorize medical care, and have received no objection.

( ) I am unable to contact the parent(s) or other person(s) having legal custody of the minor at this time, to notify them of my intended authorization.

7. My date of birth: _____________________.

8. My California's driver's license or identification card number: _____________________.

Warning: Do not sign this form if any of the statements above are incorrect, or you will be committing a crime punishable by a fine, imprisonment, or both.

I declare under penalty of perjury under the laws of the State of California that the foregoing is true and correct.

Dated: _____________________

Signed: _____________________

Notices:

1. This declaration does not affect the rights of the minor's parents or legal guardian regarding the care, custody, and control of the minor, and does not mean that the caregiver has legal custody of the minor.

2. A person who relies on this affidavit has no obligation to make any further inquiry or investigation.

3. This affidavit is not valid for more than one year after the date on which it is executed.

Additional Information:

TO CAREGIVERS:

1. "Qualified relative," for purposes of item 5, means a spouse, parent, stepparent, brother, sister, stepbrother, stepsister, half-brother, half-sister, uncle, aunt, niece, nephew, first cousin, or any person denoted by the prefix "grand" or "great," or the spouse of any of the persons specified in this definition, even after the marriage has been terminated by death or dissolution.

2. The law may require you, if you are not a relative or a currently licensed foster parent, to obtain a foster home license in order to care for a minor. If you have any questions, please contact your local department of social services.

3. If the minor stops living with you, you are required to notify any school, health care provider, or health care service plan to which you have given this affidavit.

4. If you do not have the information requested in item 8 (California driver's license or I.D.), provide another form of identification such as your social security number or Medi-Cal number.

TO SCHOOL OFFICIALS:

1. Section 48204 of the Education Code provides that this affidavit constitutes a sufficient basis for a determination of residency of the minor, without the requirement of a guardianship or other custody order, unless the school district determines from actual facts that the minor is not living with the caregiver.

2. The school district may require additional reasonable evidence that the caregiver lives at the address provided in item 4.

TO HEALTH CARE PROVIDERS AND HEALTH CARE SERVICE PLANS:

1. No person who acts in good faith reliance upon a caregiver's authorization affidavit to provide medical or dental care, without actual knowledge of facts contrary to those stated on the affidavit, is subject to criminal liability or to civil liability to any person, or is subject to professional disciplinary action, for such reliance if the applicable portions of the form are completed.

2. This affidavit does not confer dependency for health care coverage purposes.

SECTION 6910

§ 6910. Medical treatment of minor; adult entrusted with consensual power.

The parent, guardian, or caregiver of a minor who is a relative of the minor and who may authorize medical care and dental care under Section 6550, may authorize in writing an adult into whose care a minor has been entrusted to consent to medical care or dental care, or both, for the minor.

Appendix B
Sample Forms

This appendix contains examples of completed power of attorney and living wills. These are only examples of possible ways in which the forms may be completed, and are not the only manner in which these forms may be filled in.

The following forms are included in this appendix:

RECORDING REQUESTED BY

Robert Smith

AND WHEN RECORDED MAIL TO

Robert Smith
5 Maple Drive
Los Angeles, CA 90070

Uniform Statutory Form Power of Attorney

(California Probate Code Section 4401)

NOTICE: THE POWERS GRANTED BY THIS DOCUMENT ARE BROAD AND SWEEPING. THEY ARE EXPLAINED IN THE UNIFORM STATUTORY FORM POWER OF ATTORNEY ACT (CALIFORNIA PROBATE CODE SECTIONS 4400 - 4465). IF YOU HAVE ANY QUESTIONS ABOUT THESE POWERS, OBTAIN COMPETENT LEGAL ADVICE. THIS DOCUMENT DOES NOT AUTHORIZE ANYONE TO MAKE MEDICAL AND OTHER HEALTH-CARE DECISIONS FOR YOU. YOU MAY REVOKE THIS POWER OF ATTORNEY IF YOU LATER WISH TO DO SO.

I, Robert Smith, 5 Maple Drive, Los Angeles, CA 90070 _______________ (your name and address)
appoint John Jones, 123 Cedar Landing, Los Angeles, CA 90070 _______________ (name and address of the person appointed, or of each person appointed if you want to designate more than one) as my agent (attorney-in-fact) to act for me in any lawful way with respect to the following initialed subjects:

TO GRANT ALL OF THE FOLLOWING POWERS, INITIAL THE LINE IN FRONT OF (N) AND IGNORE THE LINES IN FRONT OF THE OTHER POWERS.

TO GRANT ONE OR MORE, BUT FEWER THAN ALL, OF THE FOLLOWING POWERS, INITIAL THE LINE IN FRONT OF EACH POWER YOU ARE GRANTING.

TO WITHHOLD A POWER, DO NOT INITIAL THE LINE IN FRONT OF IT. YOU MAY, BUT NEED NOT, CROSS OUT EACH POWER WITHHELD.

_______	(A)	Real property transactions.
_______	(B)	Tangible personal property transactions.
_______	(C)	Stock and bond transactions.
_______	(D)	Commodity and option transactions.
_______	(E)	Banking and other financial institution transactions.
_______	(F)	Business operating transactions.
_______	(G)	Insurance and annuity transactions.
_______	(H)	Estate, trust, and other beneficiary transactions.
_______	(I)	Claims and litigation.
_______	(J)	Personal and family maintenance.
_______	(K)	Benefits from social security, medicare, medicaid, or other governmental programs, or civil or military service.
_______	(L)	Retirement plan transactions.
_______	(M)	Tax matters.
R. S.	(N)	ALL OF THE POWERS LISTED ABOVE.

YOU NEED NOT INITIAL ANY OTHER LINES IF YOU INITIAL LINE (N).

SPECIAL INSTRUCTIONS:

ON THE FOLLOWING LINES YOU MAY GIVE SPECIAL INSTRUCTIONS LIMITING OR EXTENDING THE POWERS GRANTED TO YOUR AGENT. ____

____

____

____

____

____

____

UNLESS YOU DIRECT OTHERWISE ABOVE, THIS POWER OF ATTORNEY IS EFFECTIVE IMMEDIATELY AND WILL CONTINUE UNTIL IT IS REVOKED.

~~This power of attorney will continue to be effective even though I become incapacitated.~~

STRIKE THE PRECEDING SENTENCE IF YOU DO NOT WANT THIS POWER OF ATTORNEY TO CONTINUE IF YOU BECOME INCAPACITATED.

**EXERCISE OF POWER OF ATTORNEY WHERE
MORE THAN ONE AGENT DESIGNATED**

If I have designated more than one agent, the agents are to act ________________________________.

IF YOU APPOINTED MORE THAN ONE AGENT AND YOU WANT EACH AGENT TO BE ABLE TO ACT ALONE WITHOUT THE OTHER AGENT JOINING, WRITE THE WORD "SEPARATELY" IN THE BLANK SPACE ABOVE. IF YOU DO NOT INSERT ANY WORD IN THE BLANK SPACE, OR IF YOU INSERT THE WORD "JOINTLY," THEN ALL OF YOUR AGENTS MUST ACT OR SIGN TOGETHER.

I agree that any third party who receives a copy of this document may act under it. Revocation of the power of attorney is not effective as to a third party until the third party has actual knowledge of the revocation. I agree to indemnify the third party for any claims that arise against the third party because of reliance on this power of attorney.

Signed this ___8th___ day of __June__________________, ___1998___.

_Robert Smith_________________

(your signature)

012-34-5678__________________

(your social security number)

State of ____California__________, County of ___Los Angeles________,

BY ACCEPTING OR ACTING UNDER THE APPOINTMENT, THE AGENT ASSUMES THE FIDUCIARY AND OTHER LEGAL RESPONSIBILITIES OF AN AGENT.

[NOTARY PROVISION OMITTED]

Statutory Form Durable Power of Attorney for Health Care

(California Probate Code Section 4771)

WARNING TO PERSON EXECUTING THIS DOCUMENT

THIS IS AN IMPORTANT LEGAL DOCUMENT WHICH IS AUTHORIZED BY THE KEENE HEALTH CARE AGENT ACT. BEFORE EXECUTING THIS DOCUMENT, YOU SHOULD KNOW THESE IMPORTANT FACTS:

THIS DOCUMENT GIVES THE PERSON YOU DESIGNATE AS YOUR AGENT (THE ATTORNEY-IN-FACT) THE POWER TO MAKE HEALTH CARE DECISIONS FOR YOU. YOUR AGENT MUST ACT CONSISTENT WITH YOUR DESIRES AS STATED IN THIS DOCUMENT OR OTHERWISE MADE KNOWN.

EXCEPT AS YOU OTHERWISE SPECIFY IN THIS DOCUMENT, THIS DOCUMENT GIVES YOUR AGENT THE POWER TO CONSENT TO YOUR DOCTOR NOT GIVING TREATMENT OR STOPPING TREATMENT NECESSARY TO KEEP YOU ALIVE.

NOTWITHSTANDING THIS DOCUMENT, YOU HAVE THE RIGHT TO MAKE MEDICAL AND OTHER HEALTH CARE DECISIONS FOR YOURSELF AS LONG AS YOU CAN GIVE INFORMED CONSENT WITH RESPECT TO THE PARTICULAR DECISION. IN ADDITION, NO TREATMENT MAY BE GIVEN TO YOU OVER YOUR OBJECTION AT THE TIME, AND HEALTH CARE NECESSARY TO KEEP YOU ALIVE MAY NOT BE STOPPED OR WITHHELD IF YOU OBJECT AT THE TIME.

THIS DOCUMENT GIVES YOUR AGENT AUTHORITY TO CONSENT, REFUSE TO CONSENT, OR TO WITHDRAW CONSENT TO ANY CARE, TREATMENT, SERVICE, OR PROCEDURE TO MAINTAIN, DIAGNOSE, OR TREAT A PHYSICAL OR MENTAL CONDITION. THIS POWER IS SUBJECT TO ANY STATEMENT OF YOUR DESIRES AND ANY LIMITATION THAT YOU INCLUDE IN THIS DOCUMENT. YOU MAY STATE IN THIS DOCUMENT ANY TYPES OF TREATMENT THAT YOU DO NOT DESIRE. IN ADDITION, A COURT CAN TAKE AWAY THE POWER OF YOUR AGENT TO MAKE HEALTH CARE DECISIONS FOR YOU IF YOUR AGENT (1) AUTHORIZES ANYTHING THAT IS ILLEGAL, (2) ACTS CONTRARY TO YOUR KNOWN DESIRES, OR (3) WHERE YOUR DESIRES ARE NOT KNOWN, DOES ANYTHING THAT IS CLEARLY CONTRARY TO YOUR BEST INTERESTS.

THE POWERS GIVEN BY THIS DOCUMENT WILL EXIST FOR AN INDEFINITE PERIOD OF TIME UNLESS YOU LIMIT THEIR DURATION IN THIS DOCUMENT.

YOU HAVE THE RIGHT TO REVOKE THE AUTHORITY OF YOUR AGENT BY NOTIFYING YOUR AGENT OR YOUR TREATING DOCTOR, HOSPITAL, OR OTHER HEALTH CARE PROVIDER ORALLY OR IN WRITING OF THE REVOCATION.

YOUR AGENT HAS THE RIGHT TO EXAMINE YOUR MEDICAL RECORDS AND TO CONSENT TO THEIR DISCLOSURE UNLESS YOU LIMIT THIS RIGHT IN THIS DOCUMENT.

UNLESS YOU OTHERWISE SPECIFY IN THIS DOCUMENT, THIS DOCUMENT GIVES YOUR AGENT THE POWER AFTER YOU DIE TO (1) AUTHORIZE AN AUTOPSY, (2) DONATE YOUR BODY OR PARTS THEREOF FOR TRANSPLANT OR THERAPEUTIC OR EDUCATIONAL OR SCIENTIFIC PURPOSES, AND (3) DIRECT THE DISPOSITION OF YOUR REMAINS.

THIS DOCUMENT REVOKES ANY PRIOR DURABLE POWER OF ATTORNEY FOR HEALTH CARE.

YOU SHOULD CAREFULLY READ AND FOLLOW THE WITNESSING PROCEDURE DESCRIBED AT THE END OF THIS FORM. THIS DOCUMENT WILL NOT BE VALID UNLESS YOU COMPLY WITH THE WITNESSING PROCEDURE.

IF THERE IS ANYTHING IN THIS DOCUMENT THAT YOU DO NOT UNDERSTAND, YOU SHOULD ASK A LAWYER TO EXPLAIN IT TO YOU.

YOUR AGENT MAY NEED THIS DOCUMENT IMMEDIATELY IN CASE OF AN EMERGENCY THAT REQUIRES A DECISION CONCERNING YOUR HEALTH CARE. EITHER KEEP THIS DOCUMENT WHERE IT IS IMMEDIATELY AVAILABLE TO YOUR AGENT AND ALTERNATE AGENTS OR GIVE EACH OF THEM AN EXECUTED COPY OF THIS DOCUMENT. YOU MAY ALSO WANT TO GIVE YOUR DOCTOR AN EXECUTED COPY OF THIS DOCUMENT.

DO NOT USE THIS FORM IF YOU ARE A CONSERVATEE UNDER THE LANTERMAN-PETRIS-SHORT ACT AND YOU WANT TO APPOINT A CONSERVATOR AS YOUR AGENT. YOU CAN DO THAT ONLY IF THE APPOINTMENT DOCUMENT INCLUDES A CERTIFICATE OF YOUR ATTORNEY.

1. DESIGNATION OF HEALTH CARE AGENT. I,

Robert Smith, 5 Maple Drive, Los Angeles, CA 90070

(Insert your name and address)

do hereby designate and appoint John Jones, 123 Cedar Landing, Los Angeles, CA 90070

(714) 555-1212

(Insert name, address, and telephone number of one individual only as your agent to make health care decisions for you. None of the following may be designated as your agent: (1) your treating health care provider, (2) a nonrelative employee of your treating health care provider, (3) an operator of a community care facility, (4) a nonrelative employee of an operator of a community care facility, (5) an operator of a residential care facility for the elderly, or (6) a nonrelative employee of a residential care facility for the elderly.)

as my attorney in fact (agent) to make health care decisions for me as authorized in this document. For purposes of this document, "health care decision" means consent, refusal of consent, or withdrawal of consent to any care, treatment, service, or procedure to maintain, diagnose, or treat an individual's physical or mental condition.

2. CREATION OF DURABLE POWER OF ATTORNEY FOR HEALTH CARE. By this document I intend to create a durable power of attorney for health care under Sections 2430 to 2443, inclusive, of the California Civil Code. This power of attorney is authorized by the Keene Health Care Agent Act and shall be construed in accordance with the provisions of Sections 2500 to 2506, inclusive, of the California Civil Code. This power of attorney shall not be affected by me subsequent incapacity.

3. GENERAL STATEMENT OF AUTHORITY GRANTED. Subject to any limitations in this document, I hereby grant to my agent full power and authority to make health care decisions for me to the same extent that I could make such decisions for myself if I had the capacity to do so. In exercising this authority, my agent shall make health care decisions that are consistent with my desires as stated in this document or otherwise made known to my agent, including, but not limited to, my desires concerning obtaining or refusing or withdrawing life-prolonging care, treatment, services, and procedures.

(If you want to limit the authority of your agent to make health care decisions for you, you can state the limitations in paragraph 4 ("Statement of Desires, Special Provisions, and Limitations") below. You can indicate your desires by including a statement of your desires in the same paragraph.)

4. STATEMENT OF DESIRES, SPECIAL PROVISIONS, AND LIMITATIONS.

(Your agent must make health care decisions that are consistent with your know desires. You can, but are not required to, state your desires in the space provided below. You should consider whether you want to include a statement of your desires concerning life-prolonging care, treatment, services, and procedures. You can also include a statement of your desires concerning other matters relating to your health care. You can also make your desires known to your agent by discussing your desires with your agent or by some other means. If there are any types of treatment that you do not want to be used, you should state them in the space below. If you want to limit in any other way the authority given your agent by this document, you should state the limits in the space below. If you do not state any limits, your agent will have broad powers to make health care decisions for you, except to the extent that there are limits provided by law.)

In exercising the authority under this durable power of attorney for health care, my agent shall act consistently with my desires as stated below and is subject to the special provisions and limitations stated below:

(a) Statement of desires concerning life-prolonging care, treatment, services, and procedures:

I do not want my life to be unnecessarily and artificially prolonged with medical treatment if I have an incurable and irreversible medical condition

(b) Additional statement of desires, special provisions, and limitations:

I direct that no organ donations be made from my body parts after my death

(You may attach additional pages if you need more space to complete your statement. If you attach additional pages, you must date and sign EACH of the additional pages at the same time you date and sign this document.)

5. INSPECTION AND DISCLOSURE OF INFORMATION RELATING TO MY PHYSICAL OR MENTAL HEALTH. Subject to any limitations in this document, my agent has the power and authority to do all of the following:

(a) Request, review, and receive any information, verbal or written, regarding my physical or mental health, including, but not limited to, medical and hospital records.

(b) Execute on my behalf any releases or other documents that may be required in order to obtain this information.

(c) Consent to the disclosure of this information.

(If you want to limit the authority of your agent to receive and disclose information relating to your health, you must state the limitations in paragraph 4 ("Statement of Desires, Special Provisions, and Limitations") above.)

6. SIGNING DOCUMENTS, WAIVERS, AND RELEASES. Where necessary to implement the health care decisions that my agent is authorized by this document to make, my agent has the power and authority to execute on my behalf all of the following:

(a) Documents titled or purporting to be a "Refusal to Permit Treatment" and "Leaving Hospital Against Medical Advice."

(b) Any necessary waiver or release from liability required by a hospital or physician.

7. AUTOPSY; ANATOMICAL GIFTS; DISPOSITION OF REMAINS. Subject to any limitations in this document, my agent has the power and authority to do all of the following:

(a) Authorize an autopsy under Section 7113 of the Health and Safety Code.

(b) Make a disposition of a part or parts of my body under the Uniform Anatomical Gift Act (Chapter 3.5 (commencing with Section 7150) of Part I of Division 7 of the Health and Safety Code).

(c) Direct the disposition of my remains under Section 7100 of the Health and Safety Code.

(If you want to limit the authority of your agent to consent to an autopsy, make an anatomical gift, or direct the disposition of your remains, you must state the limitations in paragraph 4 ("Statement of Desires, Special Provisions, and Limitations") above.)

8. DURATION.

(Unless you specify otherwise in the space below, this power of attorney will exist for an indefinite period of time.)

This durable power of attorney for health care expires on _______________________________________

____

(Fill in this space ONLY if you want to limit the duration of this power of attorney.)

9. DESIGNATION OF ALTERNATE AGENTS.

(You are not required to designate any alternate agents but you may do so. Any alternate agent you designate will be able to make the same health care decisions as the agent you designated in paragraph 1, above, in the event that agent is unable or ineligible to act as your agent. If the agent you designated is your spouse, he or she becomes ineligible to act as your agent if your marriage is dissolved.)

If the person designated as my agent in paragraph 1 is not available or becomes ineligible to act as my agent to make a health care decision for me or loses the mental capacity to make health care decisions for me, or if I revoke that person's appointment or authority to act as my agent to make health care decisions for me, then I designate and appoint the following persons to serve as my agent to make health care decisions for me as authorized in this document, such persons to serve in the order listed below:

A. First Alternate Agent Joanne Jones, 123 Cedar Landing, Los Angeles CA 90070
(714)555-1212
____
(Insert name, address, and telephone number of first alternate agent)

B. Second Alternate Agent James Smith, 55 Gibson Dr., Los Angeles CA 90070
(714)555-1010
____
(Insert name, address, and telephone number of second alternate agent)

10. NOMINATION OF CONSERVATOR OF PERSON.

(A conservator of the person may be appointed for you if a court decides that one should be appointed. The conservator is responsible for your physical care, which under some circumstances includes making health care decisions for you. You are not required to nominate a conservator but you may do so. The court will appoint the person you nominate unless that would be contrary to your best interests. You may, but are not required to, nominate as your conservator the same person you named in paragraph 1 as your health care agent. You can nominate an individual as your conservator in the space below.)

If a conservator of the person is to be appointed for me, I nominate the following individual to serve as conservator of the person Scott White, 2301 Alexander St., Pasadena CA 90020

____
(Insert name and address of person nominated as conservator of the person)

11. PRIOR DESIGNATIONS REVOKED. I revoke any prior durable power of attorney for health care.

DATE AND SIGNATURE OF PRINCIPAL

(YOU MUST DATE AND SIGN THIS POWER OF ATTORNEY)

I sign my name to this Statutory Form Durable Power of Attorney for Health Care on June 8, 1998 at Los Angeles , California .

           (City)   (State)

Robert Smith
____
(You sign here)

(THIS POWER OF ATTORNEY WILL NOT BE VALID UNLESS IT IS SIGNED BY TWO QUALIFIED WIT-
NESSES WHO ARE PRESENT WHEN YOU SIGN OR ACKNOWLEDGE YOUR SIGNATURE. IF YOU
HAVE ATTACHED ANY ADDITIONAL PAGES TO THIS FORM, YOU MUST DATE AND SIGN EACH OF
THE ADDITIONAL PAGES AT THE SAME TIME YOU DATE AND SIGN THIS POWER OF ATTORNEY.)

STATEMENT OF WITNESSES

(This document must be witnessed by two qualified adult witnesses. None of the following may be used as a witness: (1) a person you designate as your agent or alternate agent, (2) a health care provider, (3) an employee of a health care provider, (4) the operator of a community care facility, (5) an employee of an operator of a community care facility, (6) the operator of a residential care facility for the elderly,
or (7) an employee of an operator of a residential care facility for the elderly. At least one of the witnesses must make the additional declaration set out following the place where the witnesses sign.)

(READ CAREFULLY BEFORE SIGNING. You can sign as a witness only if you personally know the principal or the identity of the principal is proved to you by convincing evidence.)

(To have convincing evidence of the identity of the principal, you must be presented with and reasonably rely on any one or more of
the following:

(1)   An identification card or driver's license issued by the California Department of Motor Vehicles that is current or has been issued
within five years.

(2)   A passport issued by the Department of State of the United States that is current or has been issued within five years.

(3)   Any of the following documents if the document is current or has been issued within five years and contains a photograph and
description of the person named on it, is signed by the person, and bears a serial or other identifying number:

(a)   A passport issued by a foreign government that has been stamped by the United States Immigration and Naturalization Service.

(b)   A driver's license issued by a state other than California or by a Canadian or Mexican public agency authorized to issue driver's
licenses.

(c)   An identification card issued by a state other than California.

(d)   An identification card issued by any branch of the armed forces of the United States.

(4)   If the principal is a patient in a skilled nursing facility, a witness who is a patient advocate or ombudsman may rely upon the
representations of the administrator or staff of the skilled nursing facility, or of family members, as convincing evidence of the identity of
the principal if the patient advocate or ombudsman believes that the representations provide a reasonable basis for determining the identity of the principal.)

(Other kinds of proof of identity are not allowed.)

I declare under penalty of perjury under the laws of California that the person who signed or acknowledged
this document is personally known to me (or proved to me on the basis of convincing evidence) to be the principal, that the principal signed or acknowledged this durable power of attorney in my presence, that the principal appears to be of sound mind and under no duress, fraud, or undue influence, that I am not the person
appointed as attorney in fact by this document, and that I am not a health care provider, an employee of a
health care provider, the operator of a community care facility, an employee of an operator of a community
care facility, the operator of a residential care facility for the elderly, nor an employee of an operator of a residential care facility for the elderly.

Signature: _Allison Kirman_
Print Name: Allison Kirman
Date: June 8, 1998

Residence Address: 20 Justin Ave.
Glendale, CA 90000

Signature: _Jason C. Smith_
Print Name: Jason C. Smith
Date: June 8, 1998

Residence Address: 100 Wendell Rd.
Santa Monica, CA 90010

(AT LEAST ONE OF THE ABOVE WITNESSES MUST ALSO SIGN THE FOLLOWING DECLARATION.)

I further declare under penalty of perjury under the laws of California that I am not related to the principal by blood, marriage, or adoption, and, to the best of my knowledge, I am not entitled to any part of the estate
of the principal upon the death of the principal under a will now existing or by operation of law.

Signature: _Allison Kirman_   Signature:

STATEMENT OF PATIENT ADVOCATE OR OMBUDSMAN

(If you are a patient in a skilled nursing facility, one of the witnesses must be a patient advocate or ombudsman. The following statement
is required only if you are a patient in a skilled nursing facility—a health care facility that provides the following basic services: skilled nursing care and supportive care to patients whose primary need is for availability of skilled nursing care on an extended basis. The patient
advocate or ombudsman must sign both parts of the "Statement of Witnesses" above AND must also sign the following statement.)

I further declare under penalty of perjury under the laws of California that I am a patient advocate or
ombudsman as designated by the State Department of Aging and that I am serving as a witness as required by
subdivision (e) of Section 4701 of the Probate Code.

Signature: _Alissa Wilson_

DECLARATION UNDER NATURAL DEATH ACT OF CALIFORNIA
(LIVING WILL)

I, _____Robert Smith________________ (declarant), being over 18 years of age and of sound mind, willfully and voluntarily declare as follows:

If I should have an incurable and irreversible condition that has been diagnosed by two physicians and that will result in my death within a relatively short time without the administration of life-sustaining treatment or has produced an irreversible coma or persistent vegetative state, and I am no longer able to make decisions regarding my medical treatment, I direct my attending physician, pursuant to the Natural Death Act of California, to withhold or withdraw treatment, including artificially administered nutrition and hydration, that only prolongs the process of dying or the irreversible coma or persistent vegetative state and is not necessary for my comfort or to alleviate pain.

If I have been diagnosed as pregnant, and that diagnosis is known to my physician, this declaration shall have no force or effect during my pregnancy.

Signed this _8th_ day of __June_____________, _1998_

_Robert Smith______________   Los Angeles   Los Angeles
Declarant   City   County

The declarant voluntarily signed this writing in my presence. I am not a health care provider, an employee of a health care provider, the operator of a community care facility, an employee of an operator of a community care facility, the operator of a residential care facility for the elderly, or an employee of an operator of a residential care facility for the elderly.

_John Doe_______________   Los Angeles   Los Angeles
WITNESS   City   County

The declarant voluntarily signed this writing in my presence. I am not entitled to any portion of the estate of the declarant upon his or her death under any will or codicil thereto of the declarant now existing or by operation of law. I am not a health care provider, an employee of a health care provider, the operator of a community care facility, an employee of an operator of a community care facility, the operator of a residential care facility for the elderly, or an employee of an operator of a residential care facility for the elderly.

_Jane Roe________________   Los Angeles   Los Angeles
WITNESS   City   County

The declarant _X_ is ___is not a patient in a skilled nursing facility or a long-term health care facility. The following witness is a patient advocate or a ombudsman designated by the State Department of Aging:

_Mary Carter_____________________
PATIENT ADVOCATE/OMBUDSMAN

Durable Power of Attorney for Medical Treatment of a Minor
(California Family Code Section 6910)

I, the undersigned, am the parent or guardian of _____ Billy Smith _____ , a minor, and _____ Sara Smith _____ , a minor, born on _____ January 1, 1996 _____ and _____ June 15, 1993 _____ , respectively.

I hereby appoint and authorize _____ John Jones _____ (agent) to make medical and/or dental care decisions for the above named minor(s).

This authority shall terminate on _____ February 1, 1999 _____ (date)

This power of attorney shall be "durable" and shall not be affected by the undersigned subsequent incapacity.

Dated: _____ June 8, 1998 _____

_____ Robert Smith _____
(Name of Parent/Guardian)

Phone # _____ 714-555-5555 _____ (home)
444-555-8888 (St. Francis Hotel, NY)
Address: _____ 5 Maple Dr. _____
Los Angeles, CA 90070

LIMITED POWER OF ATTORNEY FOR CHILD CARE

I/We, <u>Robert Smith and Paula Smith</u>, presently residing at <u>5 Maple Drive, Los Angeles, CA 90070</u>, as the parent(s) or guardian of <u>Billy Smith and Sara Smith</u>, a minor/minors, born on <u>January 1, 1996 and June 15, 1993</u>, (respectively), hereby appoint and authorize <u>Wilma Smith</u> (agent) to act in my/our place and stead with respect to each of the following powers:

1. To enroll said minor(s) in, or withdraw said minor(s) from, any public or private school or similar institution;

2. To employ, retain, or discharge any person who may care for, counsel, treat, or in any manner assist said minor(s).

3. To exercise the same parental rights I may exercise with respect to the care, custody, and control of said minor(s), and the discretion to exercise the same rights in my agent's home or any other place selected by my agent in his or her discretion;

4. To perform all other acts necessary, or incidental to the execution of the powers enumerated herein;

Any lawful act performed by my agent shall be binding upon myself, my heirs, beneficiaries, personal representatives, and assigns. I reserve the right to amend or revoke this Limited Power of Attorney for Child Care at any time hereafter; provided, however, any institution or other party dealing with my agent may rely upon this Limited Power of Attorney for Child Care until receipt by it of a duly executed copy of my revocation thereof. Any reproduced copy of this signed original shall be deemed to be an original counterpart of this Limited Power of Attorney for Child Care. This Limited Power of Attorney for Child Care shall be "durable" and shall not be affected by the undersigned's subsequent incapacity.

This Limited Power of Attorney for Child Care shall terminate upon a subsequent written revocation or on <u>August 29, 1998</u>, whichever shall occur first.

Dated: <u>June 8, 1998</u>   Dated: <u>June 8, 1998</u>

Robert Smith   *Paula Smith*
Signature of Parent/Guardian   Signature of Parent/Guardian

Phone # <u>(714) 555-1212</u>   Phone # <u>(714) 555-1212</u>

STATE OF CALIFORNIA   )
) ss.
COUNTY OF   )

On <u>June 8, 1998</u>, before me, the undersigned, a Notary Public in and for said county and state, personally appeared <u>Robert Smith and Paula Smith</u>, personally known to me (or proved to me on the basis of satisfactory evidence) to be the person(s) whose name(s) is/are subscribed to the within instrument and acknowledged that he/she/they executed the same in his/her/their authorized capacity(ies), and that by his/her/their signature(s) on the instrument the person(s), or the entity upon behalf of which the person(s) acted, executed the instrument. WITNESS my hand and official seal.

____
Notary Public in and for said County and State

Revocation of Power of Attorney
(No real property)

I, _______Robert Smith_______________________________________ (principal),
presently of __Los Angeles_____________ (county of residence), California, hereby
revoke that POWER OF ATTORNEY dated____June 8, 1998______________, wherein I
designated ____John Jones____________ (agent) as my agent and empowered such
agent to act as my attorney-in-fact.

Dated: _March 3, 1999___________   ________*Robert Smith*__________

                                                          (principal)

Phone # _714-555-1212_________________

Address _5 Maple Dr.______________
                _Los Angeles, CA 90070_____

RECORDING REQUESTED BY

Robert Smith

AND WHEN RECORDED MAIL TO

Robert Smith
5 Maple Drive
Los Angeles, CA 90070

REVOCATION OF POWER OF ATTORNEY
(RECORDED AND/OR REAL PROPERTY INCLUDED)

I, ___Robert Smith___________________________ (principal), presently of ________Los Angeles________ (county of residence), California, hereby revoke that POWER OF ATTORNEY dated________June 8, 1998______________, and recorded as instrument number __12345__, book __123__, Page __456__, in the county of ______Los Angeles__________, state of California, wherein I designated __________ ____John Jones________(agent) as my agent and empowered such agent to act as my attorney-in-fact.

(optional) The address and legal description of real property affected by this revocation includes: Lot 1, of TRACT 14, of the ABC Subdivision recorded in Book 9, pages 1 and 2 of Misc. Maps, County Recorder of Los Angeles Commonly referred to as: 5 Maple, Los Angeles, CA

Dated:__June 14, 1999______   *Robert Smith*_______________
                                             (principal)

STATE OF CALIFORNIA   )
) ss.
COUNTY OF Los Angeles)

On____June 14, 1999______,before me, the undersigned, a Notary Public in and for said county and state, personally appeared________________Robert Smith____________, personally known to me (or proved to me on the basis of satisfactory evidence) to be the person(s) whose name(s) is/are subscribed to the within instrument and acknowledged that he/she/they executed the same in his/her/their authorized capacity(ies), and that by his/her/their signature(s) on the instrument the person(s), or the entity upon behalf of which the person(s) acted, executed the instrument.

WITNESS my hand and official seal.

____
Notary Public in and for
said County and State

Revocation of Power of Attorney for Health Care

I,___Robert Smith___________________________________,(principal), presently of ___Los Angeles_________________ (county of residence), California, hereby revoke that POWER OF ATTORNEY for Health Care dated__June 8, 1998________, wherein I designated__John Jones________________________(agent) as my agent and empowering such agent to act as my attorney-in-fact.

Dated:_January 20, 1999_______   ___*Robert Smith*_______________

                                     (principal)

                            Phone # _714-555-1111____________

                            Address _5 Maple Dr._____________

                            ____Los Angeles, CA 90070________

REVOCATION OF POWER OF ATTORNEY FOR MEDICAL TREATMENT OF A MINOR

The undersigned is/are the parent(s) or guardian(s) of <u>   Billy Smith   </u>
(name of minor),a minor, born <u> January 1, 1995 and Mary </u> Smith, a minor,
born January 10, 1993.

The undersigned hereby revoke(s) that POWER OF ATTORNEY FOR MEDICAL TREAT-
MENT OF A MINOR dated <u> June 8, 1998 </u>, wherein the undersigned designated <u>John Jones   </u> (agent) as the undersigned's agent for
making medical/dental care decisions for the above named minor(s).

Dated: <u> January 20, 1999 </u>   <u>   *Robert Smith*   </u>
                                      (principal)

Phone # <u>714-555-1212   </u>

Address <u>5 Maple Dr.   </u>
        <u>Los Angeles, CA 90070 </u>

REVOCATION OF LIMITED POWER OF ATTORNEY FOR CHILD CARE

The undersigned is/are the parent(s) or guardian(s) of ______Billy Smith______
(name of minor),a minor, born ___January 1, 1995 and Mary Smith, a minor,
born January 10, 1993.

The undersigned hereby revoke(s) that LIMITED POWER OF ATTORNEY FOR CHILD
CARE dated ___June 8, 1998_____________, wherein the undersigned designated
_______John Jones________________ (agent) as the undersigned's agent for making
decisions regarding the care of the above named minor(s).

Dated:_January 20, 1999______   ___Robert Smith_______________
                                                    (principal)

                                       Phone # 714-555-1212____________

                                       Address 5 Maple Dr.____________
                                               Los Angeles, CA 90070

DECLARATION UNDER PROBATE CODE SECTION 4305

I,____John Jones__________(name of agent), do hereby declare that:

1. I am the agent under that power of attorney executed by____Robert Smith__________ (name of principal) on ____June 8, 1998_____ (date of power of attorney).

2. As of this date I have no actual knowledge of the termination of the power of attorney or my authority thereunder as a result of the revocation or by the death of the principal. If the aforesaid power of attorney is "durable" I also have no knowledge of the principal's incapacity.

3. My execution of this declaration is conclusive proof of the nonrevocation and nontermination of the aforesaid power of attorney as of this date.

I declare under penalty of perjury under the laws of the State of California that the foregoing is true and correct and that this declaration was executed on____June 8, 1998____ (date) at____Los Angeles, CA________(city and state).

John Jones
________________________________ (signature)

If the declarant *has* executed a Living Will (Declaration Under Natural Death Act of California):

<table>
<tr>
<td>

NOTICE OF HEALTH CARE POWER OF ATTORNEY

I, __Robert Smith__, have executed a DPAHC naming ______John Jones______ as agent. Call the following phone numbers:

    714-555-5555, 714-555-5554

I have executed a Living Will.

</td>
<td>

NOTICE OF HEALTH CARE POWER OF ATTORNEY

I, ____________________, have executed a DPAHC naming ____________________ as agent. Call the following phone numbers:

I have executed a Living Will.

</td>
</tr>
</table>

If the declarant has *not* executed a Living Will (Declaration Under Natural Death Act of California):

<table>
<tr>
<td>

NOTICE OF HEALTH CARE POWER OF ATTORNEY

I, __Robert Smith__, have executed a DPAHC naming ________John Jones______ as agent. Call the following phone numbers:

    714-555-5555, 714-555-5554
    714-555-1111 (Dr. Johnson)

</td>
<td>

NOTICE OF HEALTH CARE POWER OF ATTORNEY

I, ____________________, have executed a DPAHC naming ____________________ as agent. Call the following phone numbers:

</td>
</tr>
</table>

APPENDIX C
FORMS

This appendix includes two types of forms: statutory forms approved by the California Legislature, and generic forms for when there is not an approved statutory form. An asterisk (*) designates a statutory form.

Rather than remove the forms from this book, it is suggested that you make photocopies to use, and save the originals in the book in the event you make a mistake or need to make a new power of attorney at a later date.

The following forms are included in this appendix.

<table>
<tr><td>

RECORDING REQUESTED BY

AND WHEN RECORDED MAIL TO

</td><td></td></tr>
</table>

Uniform Statutory Form Power of Attorney

(California Probate Code Section 4401)

NOTICE: THE POWERS GRANTED BY THIS DOCUMENT ARE BROAD AND SWEEPING. THEY ARE EXPLAINED IN THE UNIFORM STATUTORY FORM POWER OF ATTORNEY ACT (CALIFORNIA PROBATE CODE SECTIONS 4400 - 4465). IF YOU HAVE ANY QUESTIONS ABOUT THESE POWERS, OBTAIN COMPETENT LEGAL ADVICE. THIS DOCUMENT DOES NOT AUTHORIZE ANYONE TO MAKE MEDICAL AND OTHER HEALTH-CARE DECISIONS FOR YOU. YOU MAY REVOKE THIS POWER OF ATTORNEY IF YOU LATER WISH TO DO SO.

I, ____
____ (your name and address)
appoint____
____(name
and address of the person appointed, or of each person appointed if you want to designate more than one) as my agent (attorney-in-fact) to act for me in any lawful way with respect to the following initialed subjects:

TO GRANT ALL OF THE FOLLOWING POWERS, INITIAL THE LINE IN FRONT OF (N) AND IGNORE THE LINES IN FRONT OF THE OTHER POWERS.

TO GRANT ONE OR MORE, BUT FEWER THAN ALL, OF THE FOLLOWING POWERS, INITIAL THE LINE IN FRONT OF EACH POWER YOU ARE GRANTING.

TO WITHHOLD A POWER, DO NOT INITIAL THE LINE IN FRONT OF IT. YOU MAY, BUT NEED NOT, CROSS OUT EACH POWER WITHHELD.

_____________ (A) Real property transactions.

_____________ (B) Tangible personal property transactions.

_____________ (C) Stock and bond transactions.

_____________ (D) Commodity and option transactions.

_____________ (E) Banking and other financial institution transactions.

_____________ (F) Business operating transactions.

_____________ (G) Insurance and annuity transactions.

_____________ (H) Estate, trust, and other beneficiary transactions.

_____________ (I) Claims and litigation.

_____________ (J) Personal and family maintenance.

_____________ (K) Benefits from social security, medicare, medicaid, or other governmental programs, or civil or military service.

_____________ (L) Retirement plan transactions.

_____________ (M) Tax matters.

_____________ (N) ALL OF THE POWERS LISTED ABOVE.

YOU NEED NOT INITIAL ANY OTHER LINES IF YOU INITIAL LINE (N).

SPECIAL INSTRUCTIONS:

ON THE FOLLOWING LINES YOU MAY GIVE SPECIAL INSTRUCTIONS LIMITING OR EXTENDING THE POWERS GRANTED TO YOUR AGENT. ______________________________________

____

____

____

____

____

____

UNLESS YOU DIRECT OTHERWISE ABOVE, THIS POWER OF ATTORNEY IS EFFECTIVE IMMEDIATELY AND WILL CONTINUE UNTIL IT IS REVOKED.

This power of attorney will continue to be effective even though I become incapacitated.

STRIKE THE PRECEDING SENTENCE IF YOU DO NOT WANT THIS POWER OF ATTORNEY TO CONTINUE IF YOU BECOME INCAPACITATED.

EXERCISE OF POWER OF ATTORNEY WHERE
MORE THAN ONE AGENT DESIGNATED

If I have designated more than one agent, the agents are to act ____________________________.
IF YOU APPOINTED MORE THAN ONE AGENT AND YOU WANT EACH AGENT TO BE ABLE TO ACT ALONE WITHOUT THE OTHER AGENT JOINING, WRITE THE WORD "SEPARATELY" IN THE BLANK SPACE ABOVE. IF YOU DO NOT INSERT ANY WORD IN THE BLANK SPACE, OR IF YOU INSERT THE WORD "JOINTLY," THEN ALL OF YOUR AGENTS MUST ACT OR SIGN TOGETHER.

I agree that any third party who receives a copy of this document may act under it. Revocation of the power of attorney is not effective as to a third party until the third party has actual knowledge of the revocation. I agree to indemnify the third party for any claims that arise against the third party because of reliance on this power of attorney.

Signed this _________ day of ____________________, _________.

____
(your signature)

____
(your social security number)

State of ____________________, County of ____________________,

BY ACCEPTING OR ACTING UNDER THE APPOINTMENT, THE AGENT ASSUMES THE FIDUCIARY AND OTHER LEGAL RESPONSIBILITIES OF AN AGENT.

CERTIFICATE OF ACKNOWLEDGMENT OF NOTARY PUBLIC

State of California   )

)

County of ___________________________)

      On this ____________ day of ____, __________ before me, ____, (name of notary public) personally appeared ____, (name of principal) personally known to me (or proved to me on the basis of satisfactory evidence) to be the person whose name is subscribed to this instrument, and acknowledged that he/she executed it in his/her authorized capacity, and that by his/her signature on this instrument the person executed this instrument.

                WITNESS my hand and official seal

____

(signature of notary public)   (seal)

STATUTORY FORM DURABLE POWER OF ATTORNEY FOR HEALTH CARE

(California Probate Code Section 4771)

WARNING TO PERSON EXECUTING THIS DOCUMENT

THIS IS AN IMPORTANT LEGAL DOCUMENT WHICH IS AUTHORIZED BY THE KEENE HEALTH CARE AGENT ACT. BEFORE EXECUTING THIS DOCUMENT, YOU SHOULD KNOW THESE IMPORTANT FACTS:

THIS DOCUMENT GIVES THE PERSON YOU DESIGNATE AS YOUR AGENT (THE ATTORNEY-IN-FACT) THE POWER TO MAKE HEALTH CARE DECISIONS FOR YOU. YOUR AGENT MUST ACT CONSISTENT WITH YOUR DESIRES AS STATED IN THIS DOCUMENT OR OTHERWISE MADE KNOWN.

EXCEPT AS YOU OTHERWISE SPECIFY IN THIS DOCUMENT, THIS DOCUMENT GIVES YOUR AGENT THE POWER TO CONSENT TO YOUR DOCTOR NOT GIVING TREATMENT OR STOPPING TREATMENT NECESSARY TO KEEP YOU ALIVE.

NOTWITHSTANDING THIS DOCUMENT, YOU HAVE THE RIGHT TO MAKE MEDICAL AND OTHER HEALTH CARE DECISIONS FOR YOURSELF AS LONG AS YOU CAN GIVE INFORMED CONSENT WITH RESPECT TO THE PARTICULAR DECISION. IN ADDITION, NO TREATMENT MAY BE GIVEN TO YOU OVER YOUR OBJECTION AT THE TIME, AND HEALTH CARE NECESSARY TO KEEP YOU ALIVE MAY NOT BE STOPPED OR WITHHELD IF YOU OBJECT AT THE TIME.

THIS DOCUMENT GIVES YOUR AGENT AUTHORITY TO CONSENT, REFUSE TO CONSENT, OR TO WITHDRAW CONSENT TO ANY CARE, TREATMENT, SERVICE, OR PROCEDURE TO MAINTAIN, DIAGNOSE, OR TREAT A PHYSICAL OR MENTAL CONDITION. THIS POWER IS SUBJECT TO ANY STATEMENT OF YOUR DESIRES AND ANY LIMITATION THAT YOU INCLUDE IN THIS DOCUMENT. YOU MAY STATE IN THIS DOCUMENT ANY TYPES OF TREATMENT THAT YOU DO NOT DESIRE. IN ADDITION, A COURT CAN TAKE AWAY THE POWER OF YOUR AGENT TO MAKE HEALTH CARE DECISIONS FOR YOU IF YOUR AGENT (1) AUTHORIZES ANYTHING THAT IS ILLEGAL, (2) ACTS CONTRARY TO YOUR KNOWN DESIRES, OR (3) WHERE YOUR DESIRES ARE NOT KNOWN, DOES ANYTHING THAT IS CLEARLY CONTRARY TO YOUR BEST INTERESTS.

THE POWERS GIVEN BY THIS DOCUMENT WILL EXIST FOR AN INDEFINITE PERIOD OF TIME UNLESS YOU LIMIT THEIR DURATION IN THIS DOCUMENT.

YOU HAVE THE RIGHT TO REVOKE THE AUTHORITY OF YOUR AGENT BY NOTIFYING YOUR AGENT OR YOUR TREATING DOCTOR, HOSPITAL, OR OTHER HEALTH CARE PROVIDER ORALLY OR IN WRITING OF THE REVOCATION.

YOUR AGENT HAS THE RIGHT TO EXAMINE YOUR MEDICAL RECORDS AND TO CONSENT TO THEIR DISCLOSURE UNLESS YOU LIMIT THIS RIGHT IN THIS DOCUMENT.

UNLESS YOU OTHERWISE SPECIFY IN THIS DOCUMENT, THIS DOCUMENT GIVES YOUR AGENT THE POWER AFTER YOU DIE TO (1) AUTHORIZE AN AUTOPSY, (2) DONATE YOUR BODY OR PARTS THEREOF FOR TRANSPLANT OR THERAPEUTIC OR EDUCATIONAL OR SCIENTIFIC PURPOSES, AND (3) DIRECT THE DISPOSITION OF YOUR REMAINS.

THIS DOCUMENT REVOKES ANY PRIOR DURABLE POWER OF ATTORNEY FOR HEALTH CARE.

YOU SHOULD CAREFULLY READ AND FOLLOW THE WITNESSING PROCEDURE DESCRIBED AT THE END OF THIS FORM. THIS DOCUMENT WILL NOT BE VALID UNLESS YOU COMPLY WITH THE WITNESSING PROCEDURE.

IF THERE IS ANYTHING IN THIS DOCUMENT THAT YOU DO NOT UNDERSTAND, YOU SHOULD ASK A LAWYER TO EXPLAIN IT TO YOU.

YOUR AGENT MAY NEED THIS DOCUMENT IMMEDIATELY IN CASE OF AN EMERGENCY THAT REQUIRES A DECISION CONCERNING YOUR HEALTH CARE. EITHER KEEP THIS DOCUMENT WHERE IT IS IMMEDIATELY AVAILABLE TO YOUR AGENT AND ALTERNATE AGENTS OR GIVE EACH OF THEM AN EXECUTED COPY OF THIS DOCUMENT. YOU MAY ALSO WANT TO GIVE YOUR DOCTOR AN EXECUTED COPY OF THIS DOCUMENT.

DO NOT USE THIS FORM IF YOU ARE A CONSERVATEE UNDER THE LANTERMAN-PETRIS-SHORT ACT AND YOU WANT TO APPOINT A CONSERVATOR AS YOUR AGENT. YOU CAN DO THAT ONLY IF THE APPOINTMENT DOCUMENT INCLUDES A CERTIFICATE OF YOUR ATTORNEY.

1. DESIGNATION OF HEALTH CARE AGENT.   I,

____
(Insert your name and address)

do hereby designate and appoint ____

(Insert name, address, and telephone number of one individual only as your agent to make health care decisions for you. None of the following may be designated as your agent: (1) your treating health care provider, (2) a nonrelative employee of your treating health care provider, (3) an operator of a community care facility, (4) a nonrelative employee of an operator of a community care facility, (5) an operator of a residential care facility for the elderly, or (6) a nonrelative employee of a residential care facility for the elderly.)

as my attorney in fact (agent) to make health care decisions for me as authorized in this document. For purposes of this document, "health care decision" means consent, refusal of consent, or withdrawal of consent to any care, treatment, service, or procedure to maintain, diagnose, or treat an individual's physical or mental condition.

2. CREATION OF DURABLE POWER OF ATTORNEY FOR HEALTH CARE. By this document I intend to create a durable power of attorney for health care under Sections 2430 to 2443, inclusive, of the California Civil Code. This power of attorney is authorized by the Keene Health Care Agent Act and shall be construed in accordance with the provisions of Sections 2500 to 2506, inclusive, of the California Civil Code. This power of attorney shall not be affected by me subsequent incapacity.

3. GENERAL STATEMENT OF AUTHORITY GRANTED. Subject to any limitations in this document, I hereby grant to my agent full power and authority to make health care decisions for me to the same extent that I could make such decisions for myself if I had the capacity to do so. In exercising this authority, my agent shall make health care decisions that are consistent with my desires as stated in this document or otherwise made known to my agent, including, but not limited to, my desires concerning obtaining or refusing or withdrawing life-prolonging care, treatment, services, and procedures.
(If you want to limit the authority of your agent to make health care decisions for you, you can state the limitations in paragraph 4 ("Statement of Desires, Special Provisions, and Limitations") below. You can indicate your desires by including a statement of your desires in the same paragraph.)

4. STATEMENT OF DESIRES, SPECIAL PROVISIONS, AND LIMITATIONS.
(Your agent must make health care decisions that are consistent with your know desires. You can, but are not required to, state your desires in the space provided below. You should consider whether you want to include a statement of your desires concerning life-prolonging care, treatment, services, and procedures. You can also include a statement of your desires concerning other matters relating to your health care. You can also make your desires known to your agent by discussing your desires with your agent or by some other means. If there are any types of treatment that you do not want to be used, you should state them in the space below. If you want to limit in any other way the authority given your agent by this document, you should state the limits in the space below. If you do not state any limits, your agent will have broad powers to make health care decisions for you, except to the extent that there are limits provided by law.)

In exercising the authority under this durable power of attorney for health care, my agent shall act consistently with my desires as stated below and is subject to the special provisions and limitations stated below:

(a) Statement of desires concerning life-prolonging care, treatment, services, and procedures:

____

____

____

(b) Additional statement of desires, special provisions, and limitations:

____

____

____

(You may attach additional pages if you need more space to complete your statement. If you attach additional pages, you must date and sign EACH of the additional pages at the same time you date and sign this document.)

5. INSPECTION AND DISCLOSURE OF INFORMATION RELATING TO MY PHYSICAL OR MENTAL HEALTH. Subject to any limitations in this document, my agent has the power and authority to do all of the following:

(a) Request, review, and receive any information, verbal or written, regarding my physical or mental health, including, but not limited to, medical and hospital records.

(b) Execute on my behalf any releases or other documents that may be required in order to obtain this information.

(c) Consent to the disclosure of this information.
(If you want to limit the authority of your agent to receive and disclose information relating to your health, you must state the limitations in paragraph 4 ("Statement of Desires, Special Provisions, and Limitations") above.)

6.   SIGNING DOCUMENTS, WAIVERS, AND RELEASES. Where necessary to implement the health care decisions that my agent is authorized by this document to make, my agent has the power and authority to execute on my behalf all of the following:

(a) Documents titled or purporting to be a "Refusal to Permit Treatment" and "Leaving Hospital Against Medical Advice."

(b) Any necessary waiver or release from liability required by a hospital or physician.

7.   AUTOPSY; ANATOMICAL GIFTS; DISPOSITION OF REMAINS. Subject to any limitations in this document, my agent has the power and authority to do all of the following:

(a) Authorize an autopsy under Section 7113 of the Health and Safety Code.

(b) Make a disposition of a part or parts of my body under the Uniform Anatomical Gift Act (Chapter 3.5 (commencing with Section 7150) of Part I of Division 7 of the Health and Safety Code).

(c) Direct the disposition of my remains under Section 7100 of the Health and Safety Code.

(If you want to limit the authority of your agent to consent to an autopsy, make an anatomical gift, or direct the disposition of your remains, you must state the limitations in paragraph 4 ("Statement of Desires, Special Provisions, and Limitations") above.)

8.   DURATION.

(Unless you specify otherwise in the space below, this power of attorney will exist for an indefinite period of time.)

This durable power of attorney for health care expires on ____

____

(Fill in this space ONLY if you want to limit the duration of this power of attorney.)

9.   DESIGNATION OF ALTERNATE AGENTS.

(You are not required to designate any alternate agents but you may do so. Any alternate agent you designate will be able to make the same health care decisions as the agent you designated in paragraph 1, above, in the event that agent is unable or ineligible to act as your agent. If the agent you designated is your spouse, he or she becomes ineligible to act as your agent if your marriage is dissolved.)

If the person designated as my agent in paragraph 1 is not available or becomes ineligible to act as my agent to make a health care decision for me or loses the mental capacity to make health care decisions for me, or if I revoke that person's appointment or authority to act as my agent to make health care decisions for me, then I designate and appoint the following persons to serve as my agent to make health care decisions for me as authorized in this document, such persons to serve in the order listed below:

A. First Alternate Agent ____

____

(Insert name, address, and telephone number of first alternate agent)

B. Second Alternate Agent ____

____

(Insert name, address, and telephone number of second alternate agent)

10. NOMINATION OF CONSERVATOR OF PERSON.

(A conservator of the person may be appointed for you if a court decides that one should be appointed. The conservator is responsible for your physical care, which under some circumstances includes making health care decisions for you. You are not required to nominate a conservator but you may do so. The court will appoint the person you nominate unless that would be contrary to your best interests. You may, but are not required to, nominate as your conservator the same person you named in paragraph 1 as your health care agent. You can nominate an individual as your conservator in the space below.)

If a conservator of the person is to be appointed for me, I nominate the following individual to serve as con-servator of the person ____

____

(Insert name and address of person nominated as conservator of the person)

11. PRIOR DESIGNATIONS REVOKED. I revoke any prior durable power of attorney for health care.

DATE AND SIGNATURE OF PRINCIPAL

(YOU MUST DATE AND SIGN THIS POWER OF ATTORNEY)

I sign my name to this Statutory Form Durable Power of Attorney for Health Care on ________________________at________________________________, ____________________.

(City)   (State)

____

(You sign here)

(THIS POWER OF ATTORNEY WILL NOT BE VALID UNLESS IT IS SIGNED BY TWO QUALIFIED WITNESSES WHO ARE PRESENT WHEN YOU SIGN OR ACKNOWLEDGE YOUR SIGNATURE. IF YOU HAVE ATTACHED ANY ADDITIONAL PAGES TO THIS FORM, YOU MUST DATE AND SIGN EACH OF THE ADDITIONAL PAGES AT THE SAME TIME YOU DATE AND SIGN THIS POWER OF ATTORNEY.)

STATEMENT OF WITNESSES

(This document must be witnessed by two qualified adult witnesses. None of the following may be used as a witness: (1) a person you designate as your agent or alternate agent, (2) a health care provider, (3) an employee of a health care provider, (4) the operator of a community care facility, (5) an employee of an operator of a community care facility, (6) the operator of a residential care facility for the elderly, or (7) an employee of an operator of a residential care facility for the elderly. At least one of the witnesses must make the additional declaration set out following the place where the witnesses sign.)

(READ CAREFULLY BEFORE SIGNING. You can sign as a witness only if you personally know the principal or the identity of the principal is proved to you by convincing evidence.)

(To have convincing evidence of the identity of the principal, you must be presented with and reasonably rely on any one or more of the following:

(1) An identification card or driver's license issued by the California Department of Motor Vehicles that is current or has been issued within five years.

(2) A passport issued by the Department of State of the United States that is current or has been issued within five years.

(3) Any of the following documents if the document is current or has been issued within five years and contains a photograph and description of the person named on it, is signed by the person, and bears a serial or other identifying number:

(a) A passport issued by a foreign government that has been stamped by the United States Immigration and Naturalization Service.

(b) A driver's license issued by a state other than California or by a Canadian or Mexican public agency authorized to issue driver's licenses.

(c) An identification card issued by a state other than California.

(d) An identification card issued by any branch of the armed forces of the United States.

(4) If the principal is a patient in a skilled nursing facility, a witness who is a patient advocate or ombudsman may rely upon the representations of the administrator or staff of the skilled nursing facility, or of family members, as convincing evidence of the identity of the principal if the patient advocate or ombudsman believes that the representations provide a reasonable basis for determining the identity of the principal.)

(Other kinds of proof of identity are not allowed.)

I declare under penalty of perjury under the laws of California that the person who signed or acknowledged this document is personally known to me (or proved to me on the basis of convincing evidence) to be the principal, that the principal signed or acknowledged this durable power of attorney in my presence, that the principal appears to be of sound mind and under no duress, fraud, or undue influence, that I am not the person appointed as attorney in fact by this document, and that I am not a health care provider, an employee of a health care provider, the operator of a community care facility, an employee of an operator of a community care facility, the operator of a residential care facility for the elderly, nor an employee of an operator of a residential care facility for the elderly.

Signature:____________________________   Residence Address:____________________________

Print Name:____________________________   ____________________________

Date:____________________________   ____________________________

Signature:____________________________   Residence Address:____________________________

Print Name:____________________________   ____________________________

Date:____________________________   ____________________________

(AT LEAST ONE OF THE ABOVE WITNESSES MUST ALSO SIGN THE FOLLOWING DECLARATION.)

I further declare under penalty of perjury under the laws of California that I am not related to the principal by blood, marriage, or adoption, and, to the best of my knowledge, I am not entitled to any part of the estate of the principal upon the death of the principal under a will now existing or by operation of law.

Signature:____________________________   Signature:____________________________

STATEMENT OF PATIENT ADVOCATE OR OMBUDSMAN

(If you are a patient in a skilled nursing facility, one of the witnesses must be a patient advocate or ombudsman. The following statement is required only if you are a patient in a skilled nursing facility—a health care facility that provides the following basic services: skilled nursing care and supportive care to patients whose primary need is for availability of skilled nursing care on an extended basis. The patient advocate or ombudsman must sign both parts of the "Statement of Witnesses" above AND must also sign the following statement.)

I further declare under penalty of perjury under the laws of California that I am a patient advocate or ombudsman as designated by the State Department of Aging and that I am serving as a witness as required by subdivision (e) of Section 4701 of the Probate Code.

Signature:____________________________

Declaration Under Natural Death Act of California
(Living Will)

I, ____ (declarant), being over 18 years of age and of sound mind, willfully and voluntarily declare as follows:

If I should have an incurable and irreversible condition that has been diagnosed by two physicians and that will result in my death within a relatively short time without the administration of life-sustaining treatment or has produced an irreversible coma or persistent vegetative state, and I am no longer able to make decisions regarding my medical treatment, I direct my attending physician, pursuant to the Natural Death Act of California, to withhold or withdraw treatment, including artificially administered nutrition and hydration, that only prolongs the process of dying or the irreversible coma or persistent vegetative state and is not necessary for my comfort or to alleviate pain.

If I have been diagnosed as pregnant, and that diagnosis is known to my physician, this declaration shall have no force or effect during my pregnancy.

Signed this_____day of_____________________________,_____.

_______________________________   _____________________________________
Declarant   City   County

The declarant voluntarily signed this writing in my presence. I am not a health care provider, an employee of a health care provider, the operator of a community care facility, an employee of an operator of a community care facility, the operator of a residential care facility for the elderly, or an employee of an operator of a residential care facility for the elderly.

_______________________________   _____________________________________
WITNESS   City   County

The declarant voluntarily signed this writing in my presence. I am not entitled to any portion of the estate of the declarant upon his or her death under any will or codicil thereto of the declarant now existing or by operation of law. I am not a health care provider, an employee of a health care provider, the operator of a community care facility, an employee of an operator of a community care facility, the operator of a residential care facility for the elderly, or an employee of an operator of a residential care facility for the elderly.

_______________________________   _____________________________________
WITNESS   City   County

The declarant___is ___is not a patient in a skilled nursing facility or a long-term health care facility. The following witness is a patient advocate or a ombudsman designated by the State Department of Aging:

____
PATIENT ADVOCATE/OMBUDSMAN

Durable Power of Attorney for Medical Treatment of a Minor
(California Family Code Section 6910)

I, the undersigned, am the parent or guardian of ______________________________ , a minor, and ______________________________, a minor, born on ______________________________ and ______________________________, respectively.

I hereby appoint and authorize ______________________________ (agent) to make medical and/or dental care decisions for the above named minor(s).

This authority shall terminate on ______________________________ (date)

This power of attorney shall be "durable" and shall not be affected by the undersigned subsequent incapacity.

Dated:______________________________

____
(Name of Parent/Guardian)

Phone # ______________________________

Address: ______________________________

LIMITED POWER OF ATTORNEY FOR CHILD CARE

I/We, ____, presently residing at
____, as the parent(s)
or guardian of ____, a minor/minors,
born on ____, (respectively), hereby
appoint and authorize ____ (agent) to act in
my/our place and stead with respect to each of the following powers:

1. To enroll said minor(s) in, or withdraw said minor(s) from, any public or private school or similar institution;

2. To employ, retain, or discharge any person who may care for, counsel, treat, or in any manner assist said minor(s).

3. To exercise the same parental rights I may exercise with respect to the care, custody, and control of said minor(s), and the discretion to exercise the same rights in my agent's home or any other place selected by my agent in his or her discretion;

4. To perform all other acts necessary, or incidental to the execution of the powers enumerated herein;

Any lawful act performed by my agent shall be binding upon myself, my heirs, beneficiaries, personal representatives, and assigns. I reserve the right to amend or revoke this Limited Power of Attorney for Child Care at any time hereafter; provided, however, any institution or other party dealing with my agent may rely upon this Limited Power of Attorney for Child Care until receipt by it of a duly executed copy of my revocation thereof. Any reproduced copy of this signed original shall be deemed to be an original counterpart of this Limited Power of Attorney for Child Care. This Limited Power of Attorney for Child Care shall be "durable" and shall not be affected by the undersigned's subsequent incapacity.

This Limited Power of Attorney for Child Care shall terminate upon a subsequent written revocation or on ____, whichever shall occur first.

Dated:_____________________   Dated:_____________________

______________________________   ______________________________
Signature of Parent/Guardian   Signature of Parent/Guardian

Phone #_______________________   Phone # _______________________

STATE OF CALIFORNIA   )
) ss.
COUNTY OF   )

On_______________________,before me, the undersigned, a Notary Public in and for said county and state, personally appeared____, personally known to me (or proved to me on the basis of satisfactory evidence) to be the person(s) whose name(s) is/are subscribed to the within instrument and acknowledged that he/she/they executed the same in his/her/their authorized capacity(ies), and that by his/her/their signature(s) on the instrument the person(s), or the entity upon behalf of which the person(s) acted, executed the instrument.

WITNESS my hand and official seal.

____
Notary Public in and for said County and State

Revocation of Power of Attorney
(No real property)

I, ____ (principal),
presently of ________________________ (county of residence), California, hereby
revoke that POWER OF ATTORNEY dated_____________________________, wherein
I designated ________________________ (agent) as my agent and empowered such
agent to act as my attorney-in-fact.

Dated:_________________________   ________________________________

                                                              (principal)

                              Phone # ________________________________

                              Address ________________________________

                              ____

RECORDING REQUESTED BY

AND WHEN RECORDED MAIL TO

Revocation of Power of Attorney
(Recorded and/or Real Property Included)

I, ____ (principal),
presently of _________________________________ (county of residence), California, hereby
revoke that POWER OF ATTORNEY dated____,
and recorded as instrument number _______, book _______, Page _______, in the county of
_________________________________, state of California, wherein I designated _____________
_________________________________(agent) as my agent and empowered such agent to act as my
attorney-in-fact.

(optional) The address and legal description of real property affected by this revocation
includes:

Dated:_______________________   ____

                                                                          (principal)

STATE OF CALIFORNIA   )
) ss.
COUNTY OF   )

On_______________________,before me, the undersigned, a Notary Public in and
for said county and state, personally appeared____,
personally known to me (or proved to me on the basis of satisfactory evidence) to be the person(s) whose name(s) is/are subscribed to the within instrument and acknowledged that
he/she/they executed the same in his/her/their authorized capacity(ies), and that by
his/her/their signature(s) on the instrument the person(s), or the entity upon behalf of which
the person(s) acted, executed the instrument.

      WITNESS my hand and official seal.

____
Notary Public in and for
said County and State

Revocation of Power of Attorney for Health Care

I,____,(principal), presently

of ____________________________________ (county of residence), California, hereby revoke

that POWER OF ATTORNEY FOR HEALTH CARE dated______________________________,

wherein I designated ____ (agent) as my agent

and empowering such agent to act as my attorney-in-fact.

Dated:_______________________________   ______________________________________

                                                                    (principal)

                                          Phone # ______________________________________

                                          Address ______________________________________

                                          ____

Revocation of Power of Attorney for Medical Treatment of a Minor

The undersigned is/are the parent(s) or guardian(s) of _______________________________
(name of minor),a minor, born _________________________________.

The undersigned hereby revoke(s) that POWER OF ATTORNEY FOR MEDICAL TREAT-
MENT OF A MINOR dated _______________________________, wherein the undersigned designated ____ (agent) as the undersigned's agent for
making medical/dental care decisions for the above named minor(s).

Dated:_______________________________   _______________________________
                                                        (principal)

                                                Phone # _______________________________

                                                Address _______________________________

                                                        ____

REVOCATION OF LIMITED POWER OF ATTORNEY FOR CHILD CARE

The undersigned is/are the parent(s) or guardian(s) of ________________________________
(name of minor),a minor, born ______________________________.

The undersigned hereby revoke(s) that LIMITED POWER OF ATTORNEY FOR CHILD
CARE dated ________________________________, wherein the undersigned designated
________________________________ (agent) as the undersigned's agent for making
decisions regarding the care of the above named minor(s).

Dated:________________________   ________________________________
                                                              (principal)

                                      Phone # ________________________________

                                      Address ________________________________

                                      ____

DECLARATION UNDER PROBATE CODE SECTION 4305

I,____(name of agent), do hereby declare that:

1. I am the agent under that power of attorney executed by _______________________________
_______________________________(name of principal) on_______________________________(date of
power of attorney).

2. As of this date I have no actual knowledge of the termination of the power of attorney or my authority thereunder as a result of the revocation or by the death of the principal. If the aforesaid power of attorney is "durable" I also have no knowledge of the principal's incapacity.

3. My execution of this declaration is conclusive proof of the nonrevocation and nontermination of the aforesaid power of attorney as of this date.

I declare under penalty of perjury under the laws of the State of California that the foregoing is true and correct and that this declaration was executed on_______________________(date) at ____(city and state).

____(signature)

If the declarant *has* executed a Living Will (Declaration Under Natural Death Act of California):

<table>
<tr>
<td>

NOTICE OF HEALTH CARE POWER OF ATTORNEY

I, _______________________, have executed

a DPAHC naming _______________________

as agent. Call the following phone numbers:

I have executed a Living Will.

</td>
<td>

NOTICE OF HEALTH CARE POWER OF ATTORNEY

I, _______________________, have executed

a DPAHC naming _______________________

as agent. Call the following phone numbers:

I have executed a Living Will.

</td>
</tr>
</table>

If the declarant has *not* executed Living Will (Declaration Under Natural Death Act of California):

<table>
<tr>
<td>

NOTICE OF HEALTH CARE POWER OF ATTORNEY

I, _______________________, have executed

a DPAHC naming _______________________

as agent. Call the following phone numbers:

</td>
<td>

NOTICE OF HEALTH CARE POWER OF ATTORNEY

I, _______________________, have executed

a DPAHC naming _______________________

as agent. Call the following phone numbers:

</td>
</tr>
</table>

INDEX

Sphinx® Publishing's National Titles
Valid in All 50 States

LEGAL SURVIVAL IN BUSINESS

How to Form Your Own Corporation (2E)	$19.95
How to Form Your Own Partnership	$19.95
How to Register Your Own Copyright (2E)	$19.95
How to Register Your Own Trademark (2E)	$19.95
Most Valuable Business Legal Forms You'll Ever Need (2E)	$19.95
Most Valuable Corporate Forms You'll Ever Need (2E)	$24.95
Software Law (with diskette)	$29.95

LEGAL SURVIVAL IN COURT

Crime Victim's Guide to Justice	$19.95
Debtors' Rights (3E)	$12.95
Defend Yourself Against Criminal Charges	$19.95
Grandparents' Rights	$19.95
Help Your Lawyer Win Your Case	$12.95
Jurors' Rights (2E)	$9.95
Legal Malpractice and Other Claims Against Your Lawyer	$18.95
Legal Research Made Easy (2E)	$14.95
Simple Ways to Protect Yourself From Lawsuits	$24.95
Victims' Rights	$12.95
Winning Your Personal Injury Claim	$19.95

LEGAL SURVIVAL IN REAL ESTATE

How to Buy a Condominium or Townhome	$16.95
How to Negotiate Real Estate Contracts (3E)	$16.95
How to Negotiate Real Estate Leases (3E)	$16.95
Successful Real Estate Brokerage Management	$19.95

LEGAL SURVIVAL IN PERSONAL AFFAIRS

How to File Your Own Bankruptcy (4E)	$19.95
How to File Your Own Divorce (3E)	$19.95
How to Make Your Own Will	$12.95
How to Write Your Own Living Will	$9.95
How to Write Your Own Premarital Agreement (2E)	$19.95
How to Win Your Unemployment Compensation Claim	$19.95
Living Trusts and Simple Ways to Avoid Probate (2E)	$19.95
Most Valuable Personal Legal Forms You'll Ever Need	$14.95
Neighbor vs. Neighbor	$12.95
The Power of Attorney Handbook (3E)	$19.95
Simple Ways to Protect Yourself from Lawsuits	$24.95
Social Security Benefits Handbook (2E)	$14.95
Unmarried Parents' Rights	$19.95
U.S.A. Immigration Guide (3E)	$19.95
Guia de Inmigracion a Estados Unidos	$19.95

Legal Survival Guides are directly available from Sourcebooks, Inc., or from your local bookstores.

*For credit card orders call 1–800–43–BRIGHT, write P.O. Box 372, Naperville, IL 60566,
or fax 630-961-2168*

SPHINX® PUBLISHING ORDER FORM

BILL TO:		SHIP TO:	
Phone #	Terms	F.O.B. Chicago, IL	Ship Date

Charge my: ☐ VISA ☐ MasterCard ☐ American Express

☐ **Money Order or Personal Check**

Credit Card Number   Expiration Date

Qty	ISBN	Title	Retail	Ext.
		SPHINX PUBLISHING NATIONAL TITLES		
	1-57071-166-6	Crime Victim's Guide to Justice	$19.95	
	1-57071-342-1	Debtors' Rights (3E)	$12.95	
	1-57071-162-3	Defend Yourself Against Criminal Charges	$19.95	
	1-57248-001-7	Grandparents' Rights	$19.95	
	0-913825-99-9	Guia de Inmigracion a Estados Unidos	$19.95	
	1-57248-021-1	Help Your Lawyer Win Your Case	$12.95	
	1-57071-164-X	How to Buy a Condominium or Townhome	$16.95	
	1-57071-223-9	How to File Your Own Bankruptcy (4E)	$19.95	
	1-57071-224-7	How to File Your Own Divorce (3E)	$19.95	
	1-57071-227-1	How to Form Your Own Corporation (2E)	$19.95	
	1-57071-343-X	How to Form Your Own Partnership	$19.95	
	1-57071-228-X	How to Make Your Own Will	$12.95	
	1-57071-331-6	How to Negotiate Real Estate Contracts (3E)	$16.95	
	1-57071-332-4	How to Negotiate Real Estate Leases (3E)	$16.95	
	1-57071-225-5	How to Register Your Own Copyright (2E)	$19.95	
	1-57071-226-3	How to Register Your Own Trademark (2E)	$19.95	
	1-57071-349-9	How to Win Your Unemployment Compensation Claim	$19.95	
	1-57071-167-4	How to Write Your Own Living Will	$9.95	
	1-57071-344-8	How to Write Your Own Premarital Agreement (2E)	$19.95	
	1-57071-333-2	Jurors' Rights (2E)	$9.95	
	1-57248-032-7	Legal Malpractice and Other Claims Against...	$18.95	
	1-57071-400-2	Legal Research Made Easy (2E)	$14.95	
	1-57071-336-7	Living Trusts and Simple Ways to Avoid Probate (2E)	$19.95	
	1-57071-345-6	Most Valuable Bus. Legal Forms You'll Ever Need (2E)	$19.95	
	1-57071-346-4	Most Valuable Corporate Forms You'll Ever Need (2E)	$24.95	
	1-57071-347-2	Most Valuable Personal Legal Forms You'll Ever Need	$14.95	
	0-913825-41-7	Neighbor vs. Neighbor	$12.95	
	1-57071-348-0	The Power of Attorney Handbook (3E)	$19.95	
	1-57248-020-3	Simple Ways to Protect Yourself from Lawsuits	$24.95	
	1-57071-337-5	Social Security Benefits Handbook (2E)	$14.95	
	1-57071-163-1	Software Law (w/diskette)	$29.95	
	0-913825-86-7	Successful Real Estate Brokerage Mgmt.	$19.95	
	1-57071-399-5	Unmarried Parents' Rights	$19.95	
	1-57071-354-5	U.S.A. Immigration Guide (3E)	$19.95	
	0-913825-82-4	Victims' Rights	$12.95	
	1-57071-165-8	Winning Your Personal Injury Claim	$19.95	
		CALIFORNIA TITLES		
	1-57071-360-X	CA Power of Attorney Handbook	$12.95	
	1-57071-355-3	How to File for Divorce in CA	$19.95	
	1-57071-356-1	How to Make a CA Will	$12.95	
	1-57071-408-8	How to Probate an Estate in CA	$19.95	
	1-57071-357-X	How to Start a Business in CA	$16.95	
	1-57071-358-8	How to Win in Small Claims Court in CA	$14.95	
	1-57071-359-6	Landlords' Rights and Duties in CA	$19.95	
		FLORIDA TITLES		
	1-57071-363-4	Florida Power of Attorney Handbook (2E)	$9.95	
	1-57071-403-7	How to File for Divorce in FL (5E)	$21.95	
	1-57071-401-0	How to Form a Partnership in FL	$19.95	
	1-57248-004-1	How to Form a Nonprofit Corp. in FL (3E)	$19.95	
	1-57071-380-4	How to Form a Corporation in FL (4E)	$19.95	
	1-57071-361-8	How to Make a FL Will (5E)	$12.95	

Form Continued on Following Page   **SUBTOTAL** ______

To order, call Sourcebooks at 1-800-43-BRIGHT or FAX (630)961-2168 (Bookstores, libraries, wholesalers—please call for discount)

SPHINX® PUBLISHING ORDER FORM

Qty	ISBN	Title	Retail	Ext.
		FLORIDA TITLES (CONT'D)		
_____	1-57248-056-4	How to Modify Your FL Divorce Judgement (3E)	$22.95	_____
_____	1-57071-364-2	How to Probate an Estate in FL (3E)	$24.95	_____
_____	1-57248-005-X	How to Start a Business in FL (4E)	$16.95	_____
_____	1-57071-362-6	How to Win in Small Claims Court in FL (6E)	$14.95	_____
_____	1-57071-335-9	Landlords' Rights and Duties in FL (7E)	$19.95	_____
_____	1-57071-334-0	Land Trusts in FL (5E)	$24.95	_____
_____	0-913825-73-5	Women's Legal Rights in FL	$19.95	_____
		GEORGIA TITLES		
_____	1-57071-387-1	How to File for Divorce in GA (3E)	$19.95	_____
_____	1-57248-047-5	How to Make a GA Will (2E)	$9.95	_____
_____	1-57248-026-2	How to Start and Run a GA Business (2E)	$18.95	_____
		ILLINOIS TITLES		
_____	1-57071-405-3	How to File for Divorce in IL (2E)	$19.95	_____
_____	1-57071-415-0	How to Make an IL Will (2E)	$12.95	_____
_____	1-57071-416-9	How to Start a Business in IL (2E)	$16.95	_____
		MASSACHUSETTS TITLES		
_____	1-57071-329-4	How to File for Divorce in MA (2E)	$19.95	_____
_____	1-57248-050-5	How to Make a MA Will	$9.95	_____
_____	1-57248-053-X	How to Probate an Estate in MA	$19.95	_____
_____	1-57248-054-8	How to Start a Business in MA	$16.95	_____
_____	1-57248-055-6	Landlords' Rights and Duties in MA	$19.95	_____
		MICHIGAN TITLES		
_____	1-57071-409-6	How to File for Divorce in MI (2E)	$19.95	_____
_____	1-57248-015-7	How to Make a MI Will	$9.95	_____
_____	1-57071-407-X	How to Start a Business in MI (2E)	$16.95	_____
		MINNESOTA TITLES		
_____	1-57248-039-4	How to File for Divorce in MN	$19.95	_____
_____	1-57248-040-8	How to Form a Simple Corporation in MN	$19.95	_____
_____	1-57248-037-8	How to Make a MN Will	$9.95	_____
_____	1-57248-038-6	How to Start a Business in MN	$16.95	_____

Qty	ISBN	Title	Retail	Ext.
		NEW YORK TITLES		
_____	1-57071-184-4	How to File for Divorce in NY	$19.95	_____
_____	1-57071-183-6	How to Make a NY Will	$12.95	_____
_____	1-57071-185-2	How to Start a Business in NY	$16.95	_____
_____	1-57071-187-9	How to Win in Small Claims Court in NY	$14.95	_____
_____	1-57071-186-0	Landlords' Rights and Duties in NY	$19.95	_____
_____	1-57071-188-7	New York Power of Attorney Handbook	$19.95	_____
		NORTH CAROLINA TITLES		
_____	1-57071-326-X	How to File for Divorce in NC (2E)	$19.95	_____
_____	1-57071-327-8	How to Make a NC Will (2E)	$12.95	_____
_____	0-913825-93-X	How to Start a Business in NC	$16.95	_____
		PENNSYLVANIA TITLES		
_____	1-57071-177-1	How to File for Divorce in PA	$19.95	_____
_____	1-57071-176-3	How to Make a PA Will	$12.95	_____
_____	1-57071-178-X	How to Start a Business in PA	$16.95	_____
_____	1-57071-179-8	Landlords' Rights and Duties in PA	$19.95	_____
		TEXAS TITLES		
_____	1-57071-330-8	How to File for Divorce in TX (2E)	$19.95	_____
_____	1-57248-009-2	How to Form a Simple Corporation in TX	$19.95	_____
_____	1-57071-417-7	How to Make a TX Will (2E)	$12.95	_____
_____	1-57071-418-5	How to Probate an Estate in TX (2E)	$19.95	_____
_____	1-57071-365-0	How to Start a Business in TX (2E)	$16.95	_____
_____	1-57248-012-2	How to Win in Small Claims Court in TX	$14.95	_____
_____	1-57248-011-4	Landlords' Rights and Duties in TX	$19.95	_____

SUBTOTAL THIS PAGE _____

SUBTOTAL PREVIOUS PAGE _____

Illinois residents add 6.75% sales tax

Florida residents add 6% state sales tax plus applicable discretionary surtax _____

Shipping— $4.00 for 1st book, $1.00 each additional _____

TOTAL _____